MIRACLE IN MOTION

Reverend Antonio "T.J." Martinez Jr., SJ
May 10, 1970–November 28, 2014
Founding President of Cristo Rey Jesuit College
Preparatory School of Houston, Texas

Viva Cristo Rey!
Viva Cristo Rey Jesuit!

MIRACLE
in MOTION

LIVING *a*
PURPOSEFUL LIFE

ANTONIO MARTINEZ JR., SJ
WITH DAVID WARDEN
FOREWORD BY JAMES MARTIN, SJ

Paulist Press
New York / Mahwah, NJ

Interior and cover/jacket photo and image credits: Frontispiece photo of T.J. Martinez, S.J. by CatchLight Group, used with permission; Cristo Rey Jesuit College Preparatory School of Houston branding and logo by BrandExtract, Designer/ Creative Director: Will Cunningham, used with permission.

Cover / jacket design by Dawn Massa
Book design by Lynn Else

Library of Congress Cataloging-in-Publication Data
Names: Martinez, Antonio (Jesuit), author.
Title: Miracle in motion: living a purposeful life / Antonio Martinez, Jr., SJ, with David Warden.
Description: New York : Paulist Press, 2017. | Includes bibliographical references.
Identifiers: LCCN 2017005800| ISBN 9780809106479 (hardcover : alk. paper) | ISBN 9780809153633 (pbk. : alk. paper)
Subjects: LCSH: Youth—Religious life.
Classification: LCC BV4531.3 .M37 2017 | DDC 248.4—dc23 LC record available at https://lccn.loc.gov/2017005800

ISBN 978-0-8091-0647-9 (hardcover)
ISBN 978-1-58768-732-7 (e-book)

Published by Paulist Press
997 Macarthur Boulevard
Mahwah, New Jersey 07430

www.paulistpress.com

Printed and bound in the
United States of America

To the students and graduates of
Cristo Rey Jesuit College Preparatory School
of Houston, Texas:

You are the miracle!

CONTENTS

Contents

FOREWORD

A Letter from Fr. James Martin, SJ, to Fr. Antonio "T. J." Martinez, SJ

November 19, 2014

Querido amigo:

Grace and peace to you, T.J.

    I write this with a full heart because I just heard that you have stopped your treatments. I know it's a good decision, T.J., and one that you made in consultation with God and the doctors, but it brings me to tears to think of your earthly pilgrimage as coming closer to an end. It's selfish of me, I know, but it does make me very, very sad.

    I also know that it's hard for you to write and call, so I'm sending this letter to you through Flavio. I wanted to say a few things to you, even though you might know them, and even though I may have said them to you before, maybe even many times.

    First of all, I'm more grateful than I can say for our friendship. I'm sure you know that, don't you? That day that you met me in Houston a few years ago, before my talk, and we spent all that time in the room talking and talking, and laughing and laughing and laughing, is something I'll never forget. I felt a deep friendship with you instantly. Instantly! And I had to ask myself, "Who is this person who I feel like I've known for my entire life?" And "Who is this Jesuit who makes me laugh so much and around whom I feel so comfortable?"

And when you took me to Cristo Rey the next day, and I saw all the amazing, astonishing, incredible work that you did, and how much people loved and admired you, and how you inspired them to do great things for God, I asked myself, "Who is this person who is such a wonderful apostle?" I don't think that I have ever met anyone who was so on fire with love of Christ, and so joyful in his Christian life. And I mean that.

Then, a year later, when we planned our "getaway vacation," since you and I were so crazy busy, and you were so kind to set everything up, and we travelled through the Hill Country on that overnight with your friends at their ranch, and we laughed and laughed again, I said to myself, "Who is this person I feel so close to all of a sudden?"

So, who is this person? Well, this person, you, are a most extraordinary creation of God, and I have been so blessed to know you, my friend. And what I most want to say to you right now is thank you for your friendship and love and support of me, and thank you for showing me what it means to live a Christian life with such joy, zeal, and courage.

T.J., the little texts and messages and e-mails that you've sent me over the past few years, praising me for my work, have been so welcomed and appreciated. It was amazing knowing that there was a Jesuit brother who supported me as much as you do. So, thank you for that too.

And you know, T.J., I've always admired you so much for your love of Jesus and for the work you have done for Cristo Rey. But in the last few months I've admired you even more, which I didn't think was possible, for the way that you approached your illness. When we spoke this summer, and you told me that you saw this as a new mission, I was speechless, and frankly I wept on the other end of the phone when you were speaking. I don't think I had ever heard anyone say something like that and it was so moving to me.

I guess we never know, until the time comes, how one person will deal with illness, will deal with a serious illness, will deal with a terminal illness, or deal with death. I guess I shouldn't have been surprised at all that you would approach it with such grace and faith. But I was surprised. You're going to be embarrassed to hear me say this, but when I spoke with you that day, it was like speaking to one of the saints.

So, what I'm trying to say, Querido, is this: it's a blessing that I can't describe to have a friend who I love so much, respect so much, and admire so much, and who shows me what it means to love God so much. Thank you for that. I will never forget it.

You know I'll be praying for you through this whole time, and beyond that, and can I ask you to pray for me too, through this whole time, and beyond that too? Your prayers will be like water for me when I am dry.

What more can I say other than I love you, always will, and am grateful to you, and always will be. And I know that we shall see each other soon.

> *With all my love and prayers,*
> *Your brother in Christ,*
> *Jim*

—Father James Martin, SJ, is editor-at-large for *America* magazine and author of *Becoming Who You Are, The Jesuit Guide to (Almost) Everything,* and *Jesus: A Pilgrimage*. Father Martin was recently appointed as consultor of the Vatican's Secretariat for Communications by Pope Francis.

PREFACE

The idea for this book was hatched at a casual dinner with Father T.J. Martinez in September 2014, around the time he had decided to forgo further chemotherapy, because the treatments were physically debilitating and medically ineffective. The hope was to live his remaining months—and the doctors said he had maybe six—in a more productive mode than was possible while undergoing cancer treatments. Part of what he wanted to accomplish was to leave a legacy of advice for "his kids" at Cristo Rey Jesuit College Preparatory School, where he had been the founding president—to leave them with a little further guidance they might need in the future, things they would have certainly discussed together had he lived a longer life and been able to mentor them as they grew to young successful adults.

Miracle in Motion became the natural vehicle to accomplish his objective. So with time now precious, we quickly went to work outlining the chapters, talking through the key points to be made, gathering the substantive materials, including hundreds of e-mails, homilies, and speeches, and then writing the beginning and the end. The team included all four Martinez siblings working together—T.J., Trey, Melissa, and Andy—along with me, an average Houstonian, who like so many others, was captivated by both the man and his mission. Thankfully, Trey had started a journal a few months earlier, which became a rich and invaluable resource, and many other friends and colleagues of Father Martinez contributed through interviews, sharing their correspondence, mementos, and memories.

While the focus of the book was ostensibly the Cristo Rey Jesuit High School of Houston, Father Martinez dreamed much bigger and envisioned a broad audience inspired by the success of his students. And, ever the cheerleader for the school, he hoped the book might generate future revenues for the school he helped start, as well as the Cristo Rey Network that pioneered the unique economic model on which it was based, which provides a self-sustaining, quality Jesuit-run college preparatory education for the underprivileged. Of course, all proceeds of this book are so dedicated.

Mission in hand, we all pitched in, but within just a couple of months, during the first weeks of November, it became clear we would not get the book finished together. Father Martinez gave us some final instructions for gathering the last of the substantive material, and too weak to help further, blessed the project and asked that we finish it for him. We have done that, editing the raw materials to conform to the chapter outline he wanted, and as best we could, to capture the voice and charismatic spirit of this bigger-than-life priest that took Houston by storm in aid of a bunch of high school students who never thought they had a chance at a better life through higher education.

We certainly felt him in the room as we worked!

—*David Warden*

Acknowledgments

I wish to acknowledge all of those who saw the opportunity to support Cristo Rey Jesuit College Preparatory School of Houston, Texas, directly or indirectly, with donations, corporate work-study jobs for the students, their time and their prayers: all students and alumni, the Initial Feasibility Study Committee, the Board of Trustees, the Cabinet, the Faculty and Staff, and all donors, volunteers, and parents— all *ad majorem dei gloriam*—for the greater glory of God.

You know I know your names, and as I try to recall the last time we spoke, I hope I thanked each of you individually again—I cannot ever thank you enough. And I know there will be many more to thank in the years ahead! Finally, of course I realize that it will take others to bring this project to fruition, and I wish to thank them in advance. I will know who you are.

—*Antonio Martinez, SJ*
October 2014

Indeed, there were others, all indispensable and far too many to name here. As Father Martinez said, he "knows who you are." On behalf of myself and Father T.J.'s siblings, our job in helping to bring Father Martinez's project to fruition was aided immeasurably by the wise advice and counsel of Father James Martin, SJ. Paul Posoli and Bee Dickson were instrumental in arranging the interviews that Father Martinez requested. Lucia Warden and Lisa and Joe Turano provided many forms of invaluable support, and Kevin di Camillo helped to shape the initial manuscript. Finally, and by no means the least, Paul McMahon at Paulist Press has been a delight to work with, and an enthusiastic, thoughtful, and creative editor as he has guided the project to completion.

—*David Warden*

INTRODUCTION

I am a Jesuit priest with a worldly problem. Six years ago, I was ordered by my provincial to start a Jesuit college preparatory high school for the underprivileged in Houston, Texas: "I know you have no school, no land, no money, no kids, and no idea how to start this process…but go get it done."

It wasn't the assignment I had asked for, but as Jesuits, we take a vow of obedience and, as a junior priest, having not yet taken my final vows, I obeyed. The poorest of the poor deserve a better life, and education is one way for them to get there; it has been part of the Jesuit tradition from the beginning. Though I felt inadequate for the job, I embraced the opportunity to help.

As it turned out, it was to be my best assignment, but it would also be my last. And that's my problem.

According to the best doctors, last March I appeared to be in absolute perfect health: a small, buff Jesuit priest dedicated to keeping fit, great blood pressure and pulse, good cholesterol, and boundless high energy. Everything was where it should be for a forty-four-year-old at the "top of his game," except for this pesky Stage IV stomach cancer that seemed to appear out of nowhere, and that the best medicines are unable to stop. I have only a few months to live, and there is still work to do.

The school I was ordered to help start is Cristo Rey Jesuit in Houston, Texas. With the help and dedication of too many to name here, in six short years, we found the land, built a contemporary school, and now in the fall term of 2014 have almost five hundred students sitting at desks and participating in corporate work-study programs that help pay for their education. The "poorest of the poor" hate that moniker and the helplessness it implies, and thus an important attribute of the Cristo Rey Jesuit model is that it requires that the students earn the elite private school education we offer on their own. Quite an accomplishment when they start from an economically challenged position, but they do it and with high academic results as well. With two graduating classes under our belts, we have 100 percent accepted into colleges, and the academic scores to garner millions in awarded college scholarships!

These students are a diverse bunch: some white, some black, some Asian, some Hispanic, and some others; some girls, some boys; and some Catholic and some not. Often, they come from broken-home environments. But they all share two attributes: poverty and a thirst for learning. They are now on their way to a better life, but I know the job is not finished. And I intended to achieve that.

The students, faculty, and supporters of Cristo Rey Jesuit have become part of my family. I feel close to them, and when a Martinez feels close to you, you better watch out! You have become part of the family, with all the good and bad that comes with that. Perhaps I would not have remained president of Cristo Rey Jesuit for much longer—who knows? The vow of obedience could have placed me anywhere. But I would have been here on Earth somewhere for these kids: as a friend as they worked through college, as a mentor in discussing their first jobs, and as a priest when they fell in love and started their own families.

When the students address me as Father Martinez, it's not just a religious title for me. I take the job seriously, and like a good parent, want to help each of them find the best path in their journey through life. But now we have to work quickly. We no longer have the time to work through life's lessons together as issues come up—it's now or never!

Miracle in Motion is my last message for the graduates and students of Cristo Rey Jesuit and for those that will follow in the years to come. So, in my last months, I began writing this book *to* them; but it is also *for* them, as they grow older. Through these pages, I want to talk to them as they work through high school and college issues, and also as they grow and mature. I want them to know me better as a person and the closer friend I would have become, and I want to share my final journey in this life with them.

I am indebted to the support of my family: my mom, dad, brothers, sister, and all the rest of my truly "all American" extended family. My brothers, Trey and Andy, and sister, Melissa, who put their own lives on hold to walk with me on the last part of my journey, are largely responsible for pushing me to this stage, along with a very dear friend and collaborator. I am forever grateful that they have all agreed to finish the project, even if I cannot. But the inspiration for this effort belongs to the students; in effect, they have given me this last assignment.

As Jesuits, one of our prime missions is to focus on the poor, but rarely have I met children in underprivileged circumstances who thought much about their status as "poor"; in fact, they don't see it in those terms, and those I have come to know in Houston over the last six years are no exception. They want what all kids their age want: the independence and skills to enjoy a meaningful life. And like all kids in any economic class, they need some directed help and guidance, just as we all did, and maybe still do.

So, I offer our story for them as they are now, but also for them as they grow into adults and eventually become the ones who will offer help and guidance to others: as parents, teachers, mentors, and as donors to good causes.

The lessons I have learned from these students at Cristo Rey Jesuit over the last six years are fundamental and universal: love, responsibility, hard work, and even the power of faith. I have been blessed to help them build the kingdom of God on Earth, and this book is my gift to the present and future students as they navigate their lives. And for me, as I travel my last months, rest assured that everyone at Cristo Rey Jesuit has helped me find peace.

It's not a perfect solution and will never be able to substitute for the personal interactions we might have shared over the coming years. But perhaps my message will help the students of Cristo Rey Jesuit remember what we accomplished together. Perhaps it will help fuel their dreams for a better life. Perhaps the story of our journey together will help others in ways we cannot yet imagine.

Mostly, it is a reminder that we don't walk life's journey alone, and there are many who want to help each of us along the way: friends, mentors, teachers, family—and yes, from time to time, even a priest.

PART I

THE STORY WILL END WELL

Tell me a fact and I will learn. Tell me a truth and I will believe. But tell me a story and it will live in my heart forever.

—North American Indian proverb

1
BUILDING THE FOUNDATION

I never got the assignment I asked for as a Jesuit priest. But the assignments I *did* get were better; they prepared me for the work we have done together over the last six years and led me to know each of you, my Cristo Rey Jesuit students in Houston, Texas.

In working hard together to prepare you to enter the world beyond your family and beyond your neighborhood, you have helped me blossom and find my true calling in life. I know that finding your own career path and purpose in life is on your mind, but be patient; you are already way ahead of schedule! The first lesson in your search is that sometimes you don't get what you want; but, as the song by the Rolling Stones suggests, you just might find that you get what you need. So, here's a bit of my story, and our story together. You'll see what I mean.

I entered the Society of Jesus—the Jesuits—on August 14, 1996, after finishing law school at the University of Texas. Just ten days after taking the Texas bar examination to get my license to practice law officially, I enrolled in seminary school at St. Charles College in Grand Coteau, Louisiana.

Yes, it was a rather big change in career path, but nobody was surprised. Everyone who knew me then knew I was now chasing my dream. Finally!

Jesuit formation is a very long process of further education, spiritual development, and service. In fact, I just completed all the steps and took my final vows in summer 2014—eighteen full, rewarding, and glorious years after starting the journey. One dream accomplished!

Along the way, I had many wonderful and joyous experiences, and met so many magnificent and talented people; but make no mistake, I was often challenged, and even sometimes discouraged. My search for my "calling in life" was neither direct nor efficient, as you will see, and even after joining with my Jesuit brothers, it took years to discover what I was meant to do. Ultimately, it did become clear—at age thirty-eight! So work hard at the task before you, but keep your mind open to opportunities, and your "mission in life" will become clear for you too.

After completing the novitiate in 1998—a two-year process—like all my Jesuit brothers, I took the vow of obedience, among other vows, and began further training, part of which involved being assigned various missions: teaching, missionary, and educational assignments. These could be anywhere in the world, and to be fair, I was always asked, "What do you want to do next? Where do you want to go?" However, I never received the assignments I requested.

Always, it seemed, my superior—my Jesuit "boss"—had a different idea about what would be best for me than I did. At each transition point in my formation as a Jesuit, I could envision various options for my next assignment. It was exciting to plot my imagined career path in the Jesuit order and make what I hoped were logical and meaningful suggestions for my next step. But I never got what I asked for. Not even once! As we say down in South Texas, I was beginning to understand what it feels like to be a bug on the windshield of life.

For example, after finishing my novitiate years in 1998, I suggested that I be assigned to Fordham University in New York; I was sent to Loyola University in Chicago. In 2001, I suggested that I be sent to Strake Jesuit in Houston to do my regency—this is a two- to three-year stage of formation where we take part in an active ministry and live in a Jesuit community. Instead, I was assigned to Dallas Jesuit. After completing regency, I suggested being sent to Rome to study theology—a fairly common assignment. But I got sent to Weston Jesuit School of Theology in Boston instead. Following my ordination in 2007, I was surprised to be assigned to attend Harvard University in order to get a master's degree in education. I embraced the program at Harvard and finished that degree in half the allotted time, and even graduated at the top of my class!

Excuse me for thinking this, but I felt that, given my obedience over the last ten years and my performance at Harvard, my next suggestion would be almost automatic: I thought I would now be a perfect candidate to teach in the law school of Loyola University in New Orleans. I knew there was a Jesuit priest retiring there, and with my law degree it seemed a natural fit for my first assignment as an ordained priest. But again they said no! The Society of Jesus had other plans for me.

Just as I was finishing my degree at Harvard in May 2008, the Reverend Fred Kammer, SJ, Provincial of the Jesuit Fathers in the South, called about a new position in Houston: the Jesuits were looking for someone to start a high school for the underprivileged in the community. I objected. I had no experience in running a school, much less starting one!

Father Kammer called me three times after that initial conversation to talk about the job. The first two calls always ended with another attempt to get me on board to found this school. The third call was different. Rather than offering me the job, he simply said, "Congratulations, you are the founding president of Cristo Rey Jesuit in Houston."

"So *this* is how the vow of obedience works," I thought to myself.

In my then twelve years in the Society of Jesus, I had learned a lot about the vow of obedience! Though I had never gotten the assignment I suggested to my superiors, reflecting on my path of formation, it is clear now that each assignment had special value for me, as each helped build the foundation needed for my first assignment as an ordained priest—Cristo Rey Jesuit high school.

I had plenty of education: a bachelor's degree in political science from Boston College, a law degree from the University of Texas (UT), a master's degree in education from Harvard, and degrees in theology from Weston. I had teaching experience too, and really liked it. In fact, many of my teachers were my heroes. I remember when I walked into the constitutional law class at UT and saw that my teacher was the legendary Charles Alan Wright. While it was an absolute privilege to be in his class, at the time I remember thinking, "Oh no, this is not the guy I want—this is not going to help my GPA!" Yet, from the moment he started teaching, he had me. He was brilliant and engaging, and he embodied everything I thought was good about lawyers, law professors, and law school. I wanted to be a teacher like him.

My love of *learning* had turned into a love for *teaching*, but leading Cristo Rey Jesuit as the founding president—not as a teacher—was not exactly the career path I had anticipated. Nevertheless, here it was before me.

It was a daunting challenge, and I had my doubts at first—serious doubts: I had *no* experience in starting a high school, much less leading one; there was no money set aside to start the school and I had no experience in raising money; and there was no land, no building, or even students or teachers identified at the beginning. We did start with a good idea for the structure of the school that had been implemented successfully in other states by the Cristo Rey Network; this school was to be the first foray into Texas. But truthfully, it seemed an almost ludicrous assignment for someone like me, and secretly I thought it might be destined to become a failure on my résumé.

So the day after I graduated from Harvard in June 2008, I headed to Houston. And once I arrived, I knew almost immediately that Cristo Rey Jesuit was just what I needed, and that it had come at the perfect time. More importantly, it was what others needed from me too.

I was met in Houston by an incredible group that had been nurturing the idea for almost two years since the summer of 2006: smart, positive, dedicated people that formed the initial feasibility committee, headed by Bob Dunn, who later became the first chairman of the board of trustees. Immediately, I was totally committed!

The Cristo Rey Jesuit College Preparatory School concept was not new. The Jesuits in Chicago had pioneered the idea in 1996 with great success under the leadership of then Chicago Provincial Father Bradley Schaeffer, SJ, and founding president Father John Foley, SJ, among many others. That led to the formation of the Cristo Rey Network to replicate the program all over the nation. Later, a discussion started among some of my Jesuit brothers about finding a place in the South for a new Cristo Rey Jesuit school—Father John Payne, SJ, Father Michael Dooley, SJ, Father Mark Thibodeaux, SJ—and they gathered others around them as they considered various cities. After some thought, prayer, and economic analysis—the usual Jesuit approach to "discernment"—Houston was selected.

My Cristo Rey Jesuit students know how it works, but for others who are interested in our story, and maybe as a reminder to you later in your life, here are the fundamentals: we combine a rigorous academic high school college preparatory curriculum with an innovative corporate work-study program that allows the students to earn much of the tuition required to fund school operations. It's a special marriage of education and business that fosters responsibility, self-reliance, and a pathway to a better life for those who cannot otherwise afford it. It's not a handout, it's an opportunity. And, as you can imagine, it's *not* easy.

Our school serves some of the lowest income kids in Houston, and our promise is simple: if you go to our school, you are going to go to college. The kids go to school longer each day, which frees up one day each week where they can work at participating corporations. The key to this project is corporate sponsorship by the businesses that hire the kids, which helps fund their tuition. That money, plus philanthropic giving that all private schools require, makes the school's educational model economically sustainable. The students get a high-quality education to launch their careers, plus a valuable, real-work experience that is an education in itself. As the students mature into successful lives, they, in turn, become philanthropic donors to sustain the effort, and experience the grace that comes from giving to others.

For these corporate participants—now numbering over one hundred in the Houston area—it can be looked at as an investment in the community: they become more than donors and corporate sponsors; they become *supporters* that take ownership of the movement when they realize how it can change the landscape of education in Houston. Furthermore, they also get real work product from these students—a true "win-win" solution. I was shocked at first to see that support came from as many non-Catholics as Catholics, but it makes sense on many levels.

We officially began in 2008. From our very capable and hardworking advisory board, the board of trustees was constituted. Now all we needed was money, jobs, land, a building, students, and teachers. We still needed everything!

Many told us it wouldn't work. Remember 2008? The country was in the middle of an economic downturn, a recession bordering on a depression. But there never is a good time to start a school for economically underprivileged children, so I thought why not now? Maybe this was economic ignorance, but I thought about the children we had identified in the feasibility study for the first class. They were real. They had names. I'd have to answer to God if we didn't begin right away and they lost this opportunity, so the decision was easy—start now!

Over the next year, it all came together. We got our first donation from the parents of one of my former Dallas Jesuit students. This was followed by a seriously large lead gift from Richard and Nancy Kinder, who were not even Catholics! We found a building just when our previous deals for land or space collapsed, and the Houston community responded with sufficient donations and work-study job commitments to get us started. So, in August 2009, the eighty students of the first freshman class—awkward in their new uniforms—and a handful of teachers opened for business. I told them at our opening assembly together that they were the future of Houston. And I meant it!

It seemed that every time we faced an impossible obstacle, a solution appeared. When we were looking for a location for the school, we had several deals (for land or other buildings on which we had made bids) discouragingly fall through. But then, suddenly the building we are now in came on the market! And just after we closed on it, Hurricane Ike hit, causing much damage—but the community pulled together and we muddled through and made repairs. In retrospect, I am amazed at how many people and things had to come together to make this project work on the demanding schedule we had set. How optimistic and fragile the plan now seems to have been. What a *risk*!

But as our chairman Bob Dunn told me many times, he thought from the beginning this school project would work; it was providential, it was meant to be. And, he added, how easily we could have missed each other! I remember Bob telling me, "Padre [as he always called me], if we had been a year earlier or a year later, we would have missed you." This was nice of him to say, but the truth is that I would have missed all of you, and that would have been my great loss.

Yes, it was hard work, teamwork, and generosity at the right times and places. But I think it was more than that; indeed, it was a *miracle*.

Timing in life can be a funny thing. It can close the door to certain opportunities, but simultaneously open up other choices, if you stay alert for them and are willing to make the effort when they are presented. We live dynamic lives, always-moving, ever-changing lives, and timing can affect who your friends are, what your profession will be, who your spouse will be, and much more.

When I began law school, my initial goal when I finished the degree was to get a job with one of my heroes, Judge Reynaldo Garza, the first Mexican-American federal judge, then sitting on the Fifth Circuit Court of Appeals in New Orleans. My dream career—maybe at that time it was the mixture of my dream and my dad's dream—was to cut my teeth in the legal profession by clerking for Judge Garza, then work at the Justice Department, and after that join my dad, Tony Martinez, in the family law practice in Brownsville.

However, my brother Trey took over the plan that seemed destined for me, and as a result, Trey gave me the freedom to explore this very different pathway. I had thought about the priesthood when I was young, and at Boston College, the Jesuits reignited the idea. Going out and doing good caught my imagination. The Jesuits are known as the soldiers of Christ and the vanguard of the Church. That spoke to my faith and sense of adventure, and halfway through law school, the call to the priesthood became a call I *had* to answer.

The timing was perfect. Trey and I just happened to enroll in law school together, and we graduated together. We have always been close as brothers, and only being a year apart in age, we have walked much of life's journey together. This was no exception—each brother helping the other to see our calling in life. I became a priest and Trey became a practicing lawyer, securing the family law business. Dad was happy, and that's important, too.

Was it random "luck"—*serendipity*—or God's will that brought us together? Maybe a bit of both, but it is clear that to find your way in this world, you need to be aware of your passion, and then listen to others as they advise you about what might be your next good move. This person could be a friend, your boss, your brother, your parents or other family members, or it could be God working through them. In my case, thank God for the Jesuit vow of obedience. It definitely helped me "listen" to the advice of others—I know *you* will do better than I ever did or could!

For me, Cristo Rey Jesuit was an assignment that I did not request. I didn't think I was qualified, and I certainly knew of others who seemed better qualified. But I was wrong. Even that law degree that I finished as I was being pulled toward the priesthood has proved to be useful in our work together over the last six years. Cristo Rey Jesuit became the assignment that defines me, and I would have missed it all if I had let fear of failure trump the wisdom and faith others had in me.

So, don't underestimate what you can do; chase your dreams, and always dream big. You have no upper limit, so be open to taking a "calculated risk" when an interesting opportunity presents itself. After all, you are the future; really, you *are*!

2
THE *MAGIS*

On reflection, the beginning of 2014 was good on many fronts. Cristo Rey Jesuit was a success by any measure, having grown in population and economic stability faster than previous Cristo Rey Network schools. I had not been the failure I feared. In fact, in Houston I was treated more like a rock star, having spread the word about the school throughout Houston's top corporate boardrooms to assure jobs for the kids, and to the salons of high society in the city to secure the school's economic stability. The celebrity status that came with the job made me a bit uncomfortable, being tugged between the dinner tables of the rich and famous and life in my Jesuit community, which was more consistent with my vow of poverty. However, such contrasts were not new for the Jesuits, who have always carried on their work in the "real world"; besides, it was necessary to make the school's economic model function. So, life was good!

Nevertheless, a life lesson was coming my way—a big one. A veritable high-speed freight train, yet unseen, was barreling straight for me! And with it, a reminder of the fragility of life, but also how strong our innate ability to find beauty and joy in what may at first seem only to be suffering. It's a lesson we may all face at some point and thus it is worth sharing.

In December 2013, I had just finished a six-month mission in Africa as part of my Jesuit formation called "tertianship," the last stage before taking final vows and being welcomed as a full member into the Society of Jesus. The time in Africa had been amazing in so many ways: broadening, deeply moving, enriching, and for me, transformative beyond my imagination. It was a time for strengthening my spiritual life and for thinking about the future. Before I left, it had been agreed that my immediate assignment on my return would be another term as president of Cristo Rey Jesuit of Houston—something that excited me greatly. But my time in Africa was also a time for reflection on how I might devote my life to the service of our Church—doing God's will—as a full member of the Society of Jesus, a process of formation that had consumed the last eighteen years. I was full of ideas and plans when I stepped off the plane on my return to Houston.

My first order of business was to track down my favorite food—a Whataburger hamburger—before celebrating Christmas Eve Mass with family, old friends, and the Houston community. While I *missed* Africa, it was also wonderful to be back, and as founding president of Cristo Rey Jesuit College Preparatory School, I was committed to taking it to the next level and to ensure the economic future of the school. I couldn't wait to get started!

The New Year started in a whirlwind of activity: reconnecting with donors and corporate work-study sponsors, cultivating new donors and sponsors for the school, making sure *all* the senior kids were on their way to graduating, getting into college, receiving financial aid, and engaging further in the Houston community. Our school motto, *Magis*—the Latin admonition of St. Ignatius to always strive "to do more" to better the world—had never been clearer to me. What more can I do for these children? What more can I do for Christ?

Then on March 25, 2014, a death sentence landed in my lap: Stage IV stomach cancer. Probably not curable and about a year to live! How quickly plans can change.

Following my diagnosis, I was in shock. Surely, there must be some mistake. I have always been a guy who loved working out and running. My routine was my joy: getting up at 4 a.m. to get in a full workout, before arriving at work by 6 a.m., where I would typically remain till around 7 p.m., when I would have dinner with some supporters of Cristo Rey Jesuit; then finally get to bed around 11:30 p.m. only to be up again at 4 a.m. and *loving* it!

News of the cancer hit me in a random way. Following the shock, there was disbelief: you know…I mean, I was only forty-four years old. This is a type of cancer that strikes men who are over eighty.

So, I thought, let's get a second opinion. But the result was the same. The hammer was brought down. There was no mistake, and the options for treatment were reduced to one: aggressive chemotherapy. Surgery wouldn't work because the cancer had metastasized throughout my body.

I was stunned. I literally went from a life of pure activity on fire with Cristo Rey Jesuit, dreaming and planning on growing it bigger, to waking up in a hospital bed being told my previous life—the one I've known for six years with Cristo Rey Jesuit—was over. Suddenly, my world became incredibly small and very, very quiet.

Yet again, it seemed I wasn't getting the assignment I had asked for! I immediately stepped down from my job as president of Cristo Rey Jesuit to focus on my health—temporarily, I hoped. And I was fierce in my resolve to beat the disease, with good friends shouting encouragement: "Life is tough, but so are you!"

However, I really had no idea of the monumental task that lay ahead, and my new world was a daunting maze: hospitals, tubes, injections, pills of all sorts, and the many side effects of trying to beat the cancer; worst of all was fatigue, nausea, and a lack of appetite. I couldn't believe I had no interest in eating. After one of the earlier rounds of chemotherapy, I felt better for a few days, and when my niece Alyssa came to visit and I spied her box of Chick-fil-A chicken nuggets, I couldn't resist them. I ate them all! But that was the lone exception.

Food repulsed me during the chemotherapy treat-ment, and now it's only marginally better—some days good, most not. It is hard to explain. I had always been a ravenous eater, and everybody knew I needed an appetite now to gain strength, and I knew that too. But now, it was like somebody asking me to grow another five inches taller—something I always wanted to do! Eating now—I just can't do it.

My family was terrific from the beginning. Everybody immediately descended on Houston. The invasion of the Martinez extended family was instant, pervasive, and per-haps overwhelming to some caught in the tidal wave. But it was love-based attention and concern, and most welcomed. My brothers, Trey and Andy, kind of moved in! I didn't like to admit it, but I needed their help in navigating this new maze of doctors, hospitals, treatment schedules, and worst of all, the debilitating side effects of the chemotherapy.

While I welcomed the company, I could see it was taking a toll on the family. Sometimes watching someone you love suffer is more difficult than the suffering itself. I couldn't imagine what my parents felt; watching a child suffer is the worst. But their presence gave me strength of mind and spirit. Comforting them made me feel better. Gradually, my attitude moved from shock and disbelief to accepting God's will and ultimately believing in his plan, no matter how difficult or seemingly impossible. I began to tell them what I believed: whatever the story, the story will end well.

Of course, we all want to live, and I am no exception. It's part of the human condition to strive for life. Professor Paul Moser at Loyola University in Chicago bookends "existence" in a way I always liked: "In that awkward phase between birth and death." But mere "existence" might not be living, and here's what I mean.

The first round of chemotherapy did not produce positive results, and it made living miserable. I was taking a round of chemotherapy every two weeks, and then the inevitable "chemo hangover" would set in, not unlike getting up after a long night of drinking with the worst hangover you can imagine: it's the kind that keeps you in bed and nauseated, with pleas to God in heaven to take you now and spare you this misery, promising all along never to drink again. Now, imagine having that every day, all day, up to ten out of fourteen days.

You can't plan around it, because the side effects hit without warning, just as the results of the medicine are hard to predict. It's just part of the "chaos of cancer"—the only thing that's certain is that everything is uncertain.

Within this context, the following question comes as no surprise: Would you chose to be on Earth for a short period, living a somewhat normal life and enjoying what you can, or would you rather extend the time based on the statistics the doctors have, but constantly battle the "chemo hangover" and be relegated to a handful of foods, mostly just chicken soup? It's a question many cancer patients face, and it became relevant for me too.

Living is more than just breathing, and the chemotherapy was robbing me of my life remaining. Not everyone responds to cancer treatments in the same way, and for me the side effects were harsh, with the gains almost nonexistent. Thus, my inclination was to stop further chemotherapy—not to end my life early, but to maximize the quality of the life I had left. Most of my close friends—both inside and outside the Church—reluctantly had to agree. I left open, of course, the possibility of becoming part of an experimental program or a miraculous cure.

Our lives are not our own, but rather gifts from God, which, I believe, we are obligated to preserve the best we can. Certainly, I am opposed to ending one's life proactively for this and many other reasons. But *my* decision was different: I chose to discontinue a medical treatment that caused more harm than good to the precious gift of life I have been given. If the medicine *had* been working, my answer would have been different, but it wasn't; the medicine was ineffective and was sucking the essence out of any life I had left.

After much thought, much prayer, consultation with my Jesuit family, and a thorough review of the medical options, I opted for a less aggressive medicine regime, but one that allows me to feel better most days, to continue my work to some degree, and yes, from time to time, to eat the food I enjoy with the friends and family I love. Now *that's* living! And it's exactly what I should be doing: preserving my life as best I can, given the circumstances.

But I did have to let go of some things; I simply don't have the strength I used to have. The focus of my life for the last six years has been the success of Cristo Rey Jesuit, and I was worried. I thought to myself, "Well, they need me." "I have all these plans to take the school to the next level." "How will they succeed without me?" But one of our strong supporters, wiser than me, put it to me bluntly over a casual meeting, with a glass of wine to soften the delivery of the message. "Graveyards are full of indispensable CEOs," he said. Wow! He's right, of course; we have hired the best administrators, the best teachers, and the best staff. I immediately understood: I was helpful, but by no means indispensable.

Consequently, in late June I formally resigned the best assignment I ever had, as founding president of Cristo Rey Jesuit of Houston—a position that deserves 24/7 attention. There is simply too much at stake. It's not the exit I had anticipated, but God has his own way of having us move on to the next chapter of our stories, and I left confident in the knowledge that the mission and the students are in great, capable hands. It was a hard decision for me, but the right one because it set as a priority the mission of the school: to work day and night to get our students into and through college, secured in their faith that Christ is their ground and their goal.

I then began to write this book for you: the graduates and students of Cristo Rey Jesuit, for your use now and as you mature in the future, and for all those who may find our story inspirational and beneficial. It's my last assignment for you as your founding president. Just the possibility comforts me that I can speak to you in the future through the medium of a book about issues we both know will come up. You can try prayer too—my door will always be open!

At first I asked myself, "How can I go from being a headliner in the city of Houston to becoming a footnote?" After all, I was the founder of the newest Jesuit high school in the nation, and had done everything in my power to make it the talk of Houston. I knew that person, but who was I without Cristo Rey Jesuit? Surprisingly, the answers came rather quickly, and for me, contentedly. Furthermore, during these last few months since my diagnosis some amazingly good things have happened to me. Yes, there *are* some positives—what I have come to recognize as glimmers of grace, things that would not have happened without this experience! Here are just a few.

I have never been closer to my two brothers and my sister. Of course, we grew up together, but for the last twenty years, we have focused on getting our education and starting our careers. We kept in touch, but there was little opportunity to get close. That all changed during the last few months, and it has been wonderful! Trey has practically moved to Houston, and Melissa and Andy are constant visitors. Trey, Andy, and I have taken to doing long walks together every day that I feel strong enough. Sometimes, we walk slowly and deliberately—often no words are spoken; other times the conversations are far-ranging from the latest jokes to serious discussions about current events, people we know, Cristo Rey Jesuit, our family, the Jesuits, and the meaning of our lives. We have relived some of our childhood exploits, filled in the gaps of the last two decades, and raised issues with each other that, only a few months ago, seemed too personal and taboo. These walks and conversations have been some of my best medicine!

I remember one walk that was hilarious and lifted my spirits as I watched the playful banter between one of my closest friends and colleagues and my sister, Melissa. We all met at what Trey and Andy had dubbed the *Camino Antonio*—the three-mile jogging path around Rice University. This time it was the whole family, and a few friends, including Father Tom Greene, SJ, with whom I had been ordained in 2007. Tom really stepped in it with my sister —maybe on purpose—and got the laughter in gear, greeting her like a long-lost friend, but calling her by the wrong name, then getting her hometown, marital status, occupation, and pet's name and species all wrong, then gleefully proclaiming, "Let's take a walk and catch up." He is an endearing soul, and wants me to join him in St. Louis this fall to help work with the men in the First Studies program at Bellarmine House of Studies. It sounds like something I'd like to do.

Then there was Trey's forty-third birthday on August 31, 2014—he's just sixteen months younger than me. I knew what he wanted, and what I wanted, too. Unless there was an outright miracle, we both knew this was the last time we would celebrate Trey's birthday Mass together. It was just the two of us. Trey was the altar boy, setting out the hosts, pouring the altar wine, lighting the candles, and getting the "choir" ready by tuning the Sonos music system to the Gregorian chant station from Pandora—a setup pioneered with wide acclaim by our brother Andy. I delivered a homily just for Trey: I prayed for him and his family, and I told him it was divine providence that he and I were together here on this day and that God has a plan for us, and difficult as it is to understand sometimes, we simply must have faith that God is behind everything, and that it is all good. Then Trey prayed for me—for a miracle cure, his only birthday wish. There were no dry eyes. At the end, I told him again, this time in a whisper, "The story will end well."

The irony is that this was the first time we had celebrated Trey's birthday Mass together, and it may never have happened but for the health issues I was now facing. The rest of the evening was laughter and good conversation with our grandmother at a good restaurant. Somehow, I felt like eating that night!

Cancer has taught me to live in the moment—to savor what I'm doing right now. When you are given just a year to live—and that's just a rough guess—you learn how precious each day is, each moment. The countdown can start to be overwhelming; you suddenly realize you are not immortal, indeed, to paraphrase my friend and Jesuit brother Father Greg Boyle, that death might *not* offer an exemption in your case! But focusing on the moment takes the time pressure off, and why not? Long-term plans are less relevant, less important. Consequently, what's happening *now* becomes a richer, more meaningful experience: each special family event, each friend you greet, each glorious sunset you watch, all seem more powerful and important—maybe because you realize it could all be for the last time. Each encounter is now a precious goodbye that might have otherwise been denied.

And one last thing that both surprised me and pleased me immensely: my cancer diagnosis has made me a better priest. I never thought I was a very good pastor. I can organize, I can motivate people to reach beyond their capabilities, I can teach, and I can give a darn good speech. But I have not always been a good *listener*, and my sister, Melissa, tells a good story about that. When I was a student at Weston, she called me to ask my input about a serious personal situation with which she was struggling. Instead of listening to her, I jumped to the answer and said, "Hold on, I just had a class on this topic. Let me get my paper." Then I responded immediately, again without really listening, "I hear you and I validate you." She was sweet about it, but gently encouraged me not to go into pastoral work!

Amazingly, the experience of cancer has made me much more sensitive to the *sufferings of others*, and better able to listen to how they cope with their burden. I am so thankful for that insight. I know I am not the only one to get an "incurable diagnosis." It happens every day at the medical center here in Houston, and all around the world. Every day, doctors deliver similar bad news. Every day, another fellow human being has to deal with the inevitable, and so do their friends and families. But if we look hard, we can see God working in all of this. New medicines are discovered, new treatments developed, more people are saved, and people get closer to one another in the process.

It's *not* a perfect world, but there *is hope*. Even when circumstances seem to change for the worse, there are positives to be found if we look hard enough, and always there is more we can do to make the world a better place! No, dealing with this cancer was *not* the assignment I asked for, but I can see God at work through it, revealing the important things in life: *Magis*—always strive to do more to better the lives of others! It's a great motto and a great way to live.

3
THE MIRACLE

I never imagined that anyone would think me worthy of a *miracle*, but there it was on the Cristo Rey Jesuit website on April 3, 2014: "Miracle in Motion! We ask for your prayers for our Founding President, Father Martinez, to the Blessed Miguel Pro—a Jesuit martyr who believed so deeply in spreading the word of Christ and to whom Father Martinez has a special devotion." I was overwhelmed.

Of course, I wanted to *live*, and still do; that's just human instinct. And the whole school praying for a miracle for me gave me such hope in the early months after my diagnosis. I was also lucky enough to live in Houston, which has a world-renowned cancer treatment medical center—people travel here from all over to be cured by our doctors. I was *fierce* in my determination to get past this "inconvenient" medical problem and back to work at Cristo Rey Jesuit, and shameless in marshaling all the forces of good to fight it on my behalf—family, friends, faith. I was *focused*. And if it required a miracle, bring it on!

On reflection, I wonder, "What was I thinking?" Just what did I not understand about the diagnosis of "incurable"?

As the weeks passed and it became increasingly clear that the best medicine was *not* working, I began to think more deeply about the "miracle" we were all hoping for—my *cure*—and began to wonder if we were missing something.

The answer was not hard to find. It was *you*, the graduates and students of Cristo Rey Jesuit of Houston. The real miracle was right in front of me!

In 2013, the first graduating class of sixty students finished, and while I was taking my first round of chemotherapy that year, our second graduating class of sixty-nine students graduated with similar success. Both classes had 100 percent acceptance to college, with millions of dollars of scholarships earned. In the fall of 2014, the school had reached a sustainable population of almost five hundred students. Working together, with a dedicated faculty, administration, and board of trustees, and generous donors and corporate work-study participants, we accomplished this in *half* the time we thought it would take when we officially opened in August 2009.

When I arrived in the summer of 2008, we had *nothing* but a good idea. We were in the middle of the worst economic recession since the Great Depression. The building that we eventually purchased was on the verge of being bulldozed and destroyed; then, no sooner had we got it, Hurricane Ike struck and caused serious structural damage. Starting Cristo Rey Jesuit in Houston, particularly at that time, was a huge risk. Many told me, "Father, that is impossible!"

But, I'm a pure optimist! As I am fond of telling you, to paraphrase St. Francis of Assisi, "The difficult we do right away, and the impossible right after."

And we did. We opened with around eighty prospective students from the poorest parts of Houston, and now we have almost five hundred. We began with just a handful of corporate work-study sponsors, and now we have close to 140. We started with just a few donors and now we have hundreds. The Holy Spirit brings me to these wonderful people. When I talk about Cristo Rey, I talk about the next generation of Catholic education, and serving those children that are being marginalized by society—and the job gets done. We focused on an area of Houston where there is a 50 to 60 percent dropout rate for the demographic we are serving—the children from the poorest neighborhoods—and we have had a 100 percent rate acceptance into college. That's Cristo Rey Jesuit of Houston—*your* school!

It wasn't an easy sale to that first class of students. They were suspicious at first, and rightly so. The story we were telling could seem crazy. Was this just another false promise tossed into the *barrio*—the idea that you can get a child who is living in poverty, and sometimes on the streets, and in four years, get them *off* the streets and *into* college? Maybe the story was too good to be true. Yet that is very much in line with our tradition of a groundbreaking Catholic education: changing the game, equalizing the playing field, changing the world, and building the kingdom.

It sounded like a hard road to travel, and many of the new prospective students for the first class were skeptical. And, truthfully, as each of you now know, it is a demanding four years. We combed the streets and talked about Cristo Rey to get that first class of kids. Andres Salgado, who became valedictorian of our first graduating class, grew up in this East side Houston neighborhood and never ventured far from home prior to high school and, at first, refused to fill out the application for Cristo Rey Jesuit. We almost missed him; we had to try *twice* to get him.

I'll be very honest, the invitation *was* indeed daunting. We were searching the streets and saying, "You're going to have to go to school for ten hours per day, you're going to have to work one day a week at a corporation, *and* your school year is going to be longer than at public school." Then we would add, "You are going to go to an academically rigorous Jesuit high school, we're going to have very high expectations, and we're going to put a uniform on you. Oh, and by the way, the *worst* of all things, we are in the state of Texas, and have no football team!" A *terrible* sales pitch! They had to trust us with no evidence, no track record.

But many to whom we gave our first pitch *did* trust us. They worked hard, and it did work! Those first kids are my heroes! As Andres Salgado told me at graduation, "Most of my life I've been confined to a four-mile radius. I'm the first one in my family to go to college, to actually graduate from high school *and* then go to college—so that's really big for me and my family." Yes, it is "really big!" Andres is attending Rice University on a full scholarship, and is majoring in computer science.

That first group of kids is now in colleges all over the country: from Rice University to Loyola University in Chicago, and from the West Coast to Loyola New Orleans and further east.

Yes, it *was* a hard sale in the beginning, but there was an early indication that as students of Cristo Rey Jesuit, you would succeed, because despite your initial skepticism and your reticence to sign up, from the first day, your excitement for this new program began to show. I remember at the beginning of the year when you were each issued your new uniforms, which includes a sweater. You were so proud of the new uniform that many of you were wearing that sweater in August! I thought, "My God! It's hot, really hot! It's a hundred degrees in Houston, and they are wearing their *entire* uniform—including the sweater! They must *want* this to work!" And there was even more to it. You instinctively knew that the uniform was the equalizer; with it you looked professional, like any other private school kid. It effectively hid what was going on in your own lives and helped give you a chance. Even though you had not yet voiced it, I could tell you were committed, that you were "all in"—just as I was. All you wanted was an opportunity—a real opportunity.

So, working together, we made this "crazy idea" work. The first class paved the way, and all of you that have followed are showing the way for many others. At Cristo Rey Jesuit, we are changing lives, and, by your example, *you* students are changing lives too. As our interim president Paul Posoli reminded me, "They get rigorous academics, the work experience, and personal responsibility. We want our students to graduate understanding the importance of being open to growth, open to justice, and intellectually fit. We *expect* everyone will live as a 'man or woman for others,' as St. Ignatius taught us. And it's not just the *students* whose lives are being changed; it's their siblings, their cousins, and their neighbors. We are having an exponential impact."

Working together over the past six years, Cristo Rey Jesuit has lived up to the expectations of those in the Cristo Rey Network and all of us who worked here in Houston to make it happen. Especially *you*, the students! Even this transition of leadership from me to a new team, I believe, has been providential, just as I now see starting this school as an act of divine providence from the beginning, with all its "impossible" obstacles.

So again, I have been reflecting on the miracle the whole school has focused on in recent months, as well as the requested prayers to Blessed Miguel Pro, and wonder where divine providence is really leading us. What is the *true* miracle?

Much has been said about my special devotion to one of my Jesuit brothers, Blessed Miguel Pro, SJ. Born José Ramón Miguel Agustín Pro Juárez on January 13, 1891, he suffered from severe stomach ailments, just as I do now! But his life came to an end on November 23, 1927, when he was executed by firing squad by the Mexican government for daring to openly spread the gospel at a time when the Church was essentially outlawed in that country. His death became a public relations nightmare for the government, which eventually helped abolish the laws against the Church. His last words as he was shot, *Viva Cristo Rey* ("Long live Christ the King"), became the inspiration for our school's name: Cristo Rey Jesuit. During his homily at the beatification Mass in 1988, St. John Paul II said, "His life of sacrificing and intrepid apostolate was always inspired by a tireless evangelizing effort. Neither suffering nor serious illness, neither the exhausting ministerial activity, frequently carried out in difficult and dangerous circumstances, could stifle the radiating and contagious joy which he brought to his life for Christ and which nothing could take away." That's Miguel Pro—that's enough for me!

We shared a cultural background, we shared a brotherhood, and we shared an optimistic view of life for what could be accomplished in the face of challenging odds. For me, Father Pro was an inspiration as we *all* worked together to build Cristo Rey Jesuit of Houston these past years. In many ways, the miracle of the school, and the miracle of you, belongs to him.

Divine providence has also been at work in each of *you*. Other schools had already given up on many of you who came to Cristo Rey. But your academic progress has been *amazing*. Many thought you couldn't do it; but yes, you can. And you did! Some of you have done so well that you began taking *sophomore* classes in your freshman year! Nobody thought that could happen, but it is happening. Our program shows what you kids can do when somebody believes in you. And the jobs: the jobs allow you students who have grown up in the toughest neighborhoods and come from the most broken families to reimagine yourselves as future business leaders and future family leaders.

It's almost like pressing a reset button on your mind. It ignites a positive potential, a "divine spark" that I believe exists in every child.

Just days before my cancer diagnosis, I had the opportunity to address the entire student body and remind you of our heritage. This is what I told you and the others in the audience: "We did the impossible five and a half years ago, and many people wondered, '*Why* did you do it? *Why* would you start a school? *Why* change the model of how you finance that school? And why go after, in my mind, the best children in this city?' And my response then was, 'All I have to do is look at the audience, and I give you 436 reasons why we started Cristo Rey Jesuit.'"

My response today, some six months later, is the same, except the "number of reasons"—the student body size—has only grown larger!

Cristo Rey Jesuit is really a ministry of outreach to those people who need a "hand-up"—*not* a "hand-out"—as well as some books, some tuition, the playing field leveled just a bit, and an opportunity to succeed, where they, the *students*, invest in their own futures by rigorous attention to academics and working to pay for much of the costs. And, in a beautiful way, it has affected the Catholic community and those beyond it. We started with the idea that it would all be worthwhile *if* you can save just one child. But the wonderful Jewish community, which has been so supportive, has a better saying: "Save one child…and you save the world." So let's save five hundred worlds, and more!

My dream is that this is only the beginning, that Cristo Rey Jesuit becomes one of many in this community that is reaching the children that need us the most. And that you, the students and graduates, become an inspiration to others who face adversity and obstacles. Truthfully, my cancer seems far less important.

My life may not be *long*, but it has been *full*—because of *you*. As I have been saying now for months, and truly believe, *The story will end well*. You are my pride and joy, you are the highlight of my life, and I will live and die with my favorite story being you and this school. You are the miracle!

PART II

THE IMPORTANCE OF EDUCATION

Consider your origin. You were not formed to live like brutes but to follow virtue and knowledge.

—Dante, *Inferno*, XXVI, I.116–20

4

IT'S A JESUIT THING

Like it or not, believe it or not, a Spanish soldier born in 1491 brought us all together. Without him, perhaps there would be no Cristo Rey Jesuit College Preparatory School in Houston—or anywhere else, for that matter.

Íñigo López de Loyola—now known more commonly as St. Ignatius of Loyola—a soldier from the Basque region of northern Spain, founded the Jesuit Order on September 27, 1540, with the approval of Pope Paul III. But it wasn't obvious for much of his life that it would happen at all.

Ignatius was very much like you and me for the first part of his life. He had some talents and many faults. He became an accomplished soldier, fancied himself attractive to women, and is rumored to have "played the field" even to the point of fathering a child out of wedlock (though this legend has never been proven). Some biographers even mention arrest records, allegedly for bar fighting. None of that is particularly surprising for a soldier of that time, or even now. And in truth, there have been others, both before and after Ignatius (most notably St. Augustine, St. Norbert, and St. Francis), who did the same, and worse, before they became priests.

But Ignatius not only became a priest, he became a *saint*. His story is worth knowing because it demonstrates so clearly how we *all* can change the course of our lives.

You too can possibly become a saint, and if not that, at the very least a happy, successful, and productive person. As the Franciscans are so fond of saying, "Saints are just sinners who kept on trying!"

So, stay with me through this short narrative and trust me: this story *is* relevant to our lives today. Ignatius had some great ideas, and great ideas are hard to stop! And one of those is the story of Jesuit education.

My intention is not to bury you under the reams of scholarship on the role of education in the Jesuit order, though some of you may find that interesting to study on your own at some point. Rather, our discussion here is simply to shed some light on the rich educational tradition of which you are a continuing and vibrant part—from the sixteenth-century European beginnings to the twenty-first century global phenomenon that includes Cristo Rey Jesuit of Houston.

The turning point for Ignatius came at the age of thirty, when he was injured on the battlefield, and during his convalescence, he slowly discovered a passion that would transform his life—along with mine, and yours too! Ignatius did not know immediately where his new life would lead him; he was just sure that his old life was not ultimately fulfilling. He had apparently had enough of professional fighting as a career soldier, and of chasing women in his free time. So, he began anew, feeling his way without much worldly guidance, to a religious life that ultimately distinguished itself as focused on education and missionary work throughout the world.

Ignatius soon realized that his new life needed a new educational foundation. What he had learned as a soldier was useful, to be sure: leadership, willingness to take a risk, strategic thinking. But he needed *more* to accomplish his goals in his new endeavor in the Church. Thus, Ignatius went to study at the premier formal educational institution of his time, the University of Paris. While studying in Paris and writing what would become the foundational document of his new religious life, *The Spiritual Exercises*, he met a group of men that would ultimately form the core of his new religious order, the Society of Jesus. You see, things have a way of working out when you are on the right track!

On August 15, 1534, Ignatius and six other students at the University of Paris met in the crypt of the church of Saint-Pierre de Montmartre, just outside Paris, and professed vows of poverty, chastity, and obedience in service to the Church. Thus was born the Society of Jesus, commonly called the "Jesuits," declaring in their native Spanish an invitation to all: *todo el que quiera military para Dios*, "whoever desires to serve as a soldier of God." This core group grew in number, trained, and became ordained as priests in the Catholic Church. Six years later, the Jesuit order became official with the approval of Pope Paul III and grew rapidly.

These men of the nascent Jesuit order also adopted an additional fourth vow couched in terms of loyalty to the pope, but that also set their vision as missionaries for the faith: "I further promise a special obedience to the Sovereign Pontiff in regard to the missions according to the same apostolic letters and the Constitutions." Not to dig too deeply here, for there are endless scholarly discussions on this vow, but I have always been comfortable with the notion that the fourth vow means that members of the Jesuit order make themselves available to travel or live *anywhere* in the world in the service of the Church, and that such work shall include any "mission" or "assignment" directed exclusively by the pope, whether specifically directed to travel abroad or to adhere to a teaching of the Church. Regardless of how one interprets the original intentions of this fourth vow, it is clear that the early Jesuits identified with doing their work in the far reaches of the globe as a focus—indeed, they were true "soldiers of God."

As if to prove the point, one of the original Jesuits, St. Francis Xavier, became the first Jesuit missionary, leaving for India in 1541, just after the order was officially approved. He never returned to Europe, but continued his work in India, Japan, and China until his death in 1552. Thus, the early foundation for the missionary focus of the Jesuit order was in place, and grew from there in service to the Church and for the greater good.

Incidentally, and as a cautionary note to all of you on your way to college, Francis, quite by accident, was a college roommate of Ignatius at the University of Paris, where they first met. Francis came to Paris with no intention of joining religious life, but as fate would have it, ended up following Ignatius, even becoming a cofounder of the Society of Jesus. According to legend, Francis resisted the arguments of Ignatius until Ignatius reportedly posed the question from Scripture, "What will it profit a man to gain the whole world, and lose his own soul?" Francis apparently had no ready answer, and the rest, as they say, is history. Ordained a priest, Francis traveled the world in his ministry, died and was buried in India, and was canonized a saint in 1622. So, pick your college roommate carefully!

While the Jesuits identified a missionary focus early in their history, how did they become associated with *educational* work all over the world? Many scholars have spent years analyzing the historical period to show how the *ministry of education* evolved in the Jesuit order, but for our purposes a "sound-bite" answer will do.

The Jesuits were a product of their time, and like many of us, they responded to the events of the day. Education wasn't necessarily a key part of their plan at the very beginning, but it quickly became so. The "soldiers of God" served the Church in the middle of the sixteenth-century turmoil of the Counter Reformation—helping to bring back to the Church many of those who had been alienated by the internal corruption and spiritual fatigue pervasive at the time. They did that, in part, by helping to better educate the clergy.

But that was only part of the answer. A key objective of the Jesuit order was to develop an internal sense of purpose derived directly from the *Spiritual Exercises of St. Ignatius*, which would instill the intellectual freedom to follow one's dreams. This was accomplished, in part, through education. And then there was also a practical aspect: educating people who would later hold important commercial, political, and religious positions would place the order at the core of civilized life, and as a result, it would be better able to promote the common good.

Thus began the ministry of education wherever it was needed or, as often happened, was requested. The first Jesuit school was started in Messina, Sicily, in 1548, at the request of a group of parents who wanted their sons educated, and who were willing to put up the room and board to entice a group of Jesuit priests to the job. The school was a success, and the process repeated itself such that by the time Ignatius died some eight years later, the Jesuits were running over seventy colleges on three continents.

Of importance from the beginning was that Jesuit schools be accessible to "rich and poor alike," and open to students of *every* social class. Thus, Ignatius sought to have them endowed financially so that *no* tuition was charged. This feature gradually disappeared over the ensuing centuries, but you at Cristo Rey Jesuit can be proud of the fact that we have found a way to rejuvenate these original principles from the earliest Jesuit schools by the corporate work-study program that each of you participates in that helps pay the cost of your education.

Quality education, accessible to rich and poor alike, open to every social class is an admirable objective! An objective we still champion today.

Over time, the Jesuits developed a specific curriculum that encompassed both the new humanism of the Renaissance and the older medieval "university," which focused on theology, science, law, medicine, and the arts. Thus, the Jesuit schools went beyond the religious instruction of the Catholic Church, to include classical literature, poetry, philosophy, science, the arts, Greek, Latin, and many other languages.

In addition, and perhaps arising from the Jesuit's global reach from the beginning, the pedagogy demanded respect for the religious views of those *outside* Christianity. This Jesuit tradition remains in place today. It is perhaps most recently evident in Pope Francis, the first Jesuit pope, who has lived a life of religious tolerance, reaching out to Jews, Muslims, other Christian faiths, and even nonbelievers, when he said, "We all know that mutual respect is fundamental in any human relationship, especially among people who profess religious belief." Searching for God in *all* things is a fundamental aspect of the Jesuit approach, which surely informed their teaching from the beginning.

Thus, the foundation for what we now know as a "Jesuit education" was laid early on, and the results were outstanding. Today, Jesuit colleges, universities, and schools operate in over one hundred countries around the world. But it wasn't always easy.

In fact, in the almost 475-year history of the Jesuits, their ministry of operating schools throughout the world has often been met with distrust, conflict, and destruction. Jesuit priests have been killed for intruding into foreign lands, shot as suspected spies, imprisoned, and executed as a danger to the status quo. Indeed, by 1773, when the

Jesuits were operating some eight hundred schools around the world, secular opposition to the influence of the Society pressured Pope Clement XIV to suppress Jesuit operations in most countries. This effectively wiped out most of the Jesuit international network. But the order was reinstated by Pope Pius VII in 1814 and has grown to the global institution we have today. Along the way, it has influenced many other religious orders, societies, and congregations to take on the ministry of education as a principal focus.

Because of the power that comes with knowledge and thinking for oneself, a broad education, like that offered by the Jesuit curriculum, was often viewed by the ruling class as a danger to their incumbency. That is even true today in some countries where freedom to learn is circumscribed by banning books, Internet censorship, and a government-controlled media. It is true in other places with respect to restricting women from education or selectively banning certain subject matters. Just as in the past, in today's world the Jesuit ministry of education—and others who have joined in that ministry—is often met with opposition, and sometimes danger.

For example, in America, there was a time when some politicians tried to stop the ministry of education as practiced by the Jesuit order and others. In 1922, the state of Oregon enacted a statute called the Compulsory Education Act, making it a *criminal* violation for any parent or guardian of a child between the ages of eight and sixteen if they "fail or neglect or refuse to send such child to a public school." Of course, the net result of this law would have been to completely wipe out all privately run schools, including those operated by religious orders, such as the Jesuits. The federal district court sided with the governor of Oregon in effectively instituting a ban on private schools, but fortunately the Supreme Court of the United States found the Oregon law unconstitutional.

Here's how a lawyer would tell the story. In *Pierce v. Society of the Sisters of the Holy Names of Jesus and Mary*, 268 U.S. 510 (1925), the Court held that "the Act of 1922 unreasonably interferes with the liberty of parents and guardians to direct the upbringing and education of children under their control" (534–5). The Court went on to say, "The child is not the mere creature of the state; those who nurture him and direct his destiny have the right, coupled with the high duty, to recognize and prepare him for additional obligations" (535). Thus, the Oregon law was defeated, and with its decision, the Supreme Court effectively prohibited any other state from attempting to institute a similar ban on privately operated educational institutions.

So, don't let anyone tell you that lawyers cannot do good deeds! I am a lawyer, as well as a priest, and my family is full of lawyers, including my dad and both of my brothers. The world presents ample opportunities for all of us to work for the common good!

Thus, despite the challenges from many quarters over the centuries, the ministry of education thrives today in the Jesuit order, as well as many others. In America alone, the Jesuits run twenty-eight colleges and universities and over eighty high schools. Cristo Rey Jesuit, as a model to provide a high-quality college preparatory education for the underprivileged in urban areas, was begun by the Jesuits in 1996, and today—as of this writing—there are thirty-two such high schools under the umbrella of the Cristo Rey Network, with Cristo Rey Jesuit of Houston as one of the more recent, and the model is catching on with other group sponsors as well.

The Jesuits could have chosen an easier ministry than education, but "soldiers of God" are not afraid of a challenge.

Education is perhaps the most powerful tool of a free society, and that is true no matter *who* brings it to you: the Jesuits or the many fine schools throughout the world today, run by other distinguished organizations.

Now, almost 475 years later, the Jesuit ministry continues in Houston, Texas, where it is personal with me and with all of you, for it has brought us together and has changed our lives. Consequently, a quality education is a "high duty." It should be open to all; it is worth fighting for, and it is worth working hard to achieve. Indeed, it is a Jesuit thing!

5
FIND YOUR PASSION

"Give a man a fish and you feed him for a day. Teach a man to fish and you feed him for a lifetime." This Chinese proverb is often attributed to the philosopher Lao-tzu, who lived nearly 2,700 years ago, around 600 BC (before Christ). I would never have known that proverb if I had not received a quality education. Believe me, we did not sit around reciting Chinese proverbs in Brownsville, Texas, when we were kids! I learned it much later.

However, what this ancient Chinese proverb tells us is important to our lives today, and important to each of you in charting a better life through education. So, let's talk about that for a few minutes, since the topic of *your* education is where *our* relationship started. A quality education is *not* going to be the answer to *all* your problems in life; but trust me, it is a key part of the *solution*.

As friends, we can face a simple fact: I am a short, skinny guy. I always wished that I wasn't, but I am stuck with the body I came with at birth. So, my road out of the *barrio* was never going to be as a great and highly paid sports hero (except perhaps as a jockey!). But we are all given a brain, and through work and study we can make it serve us better. Therefore, education was my ticket to a better life, as it is for most of you, too.

Recall what I said at the first graduation ceremony at Cristo Rey Jesuit: "Every so often, in the pages of Houston's history, moments evolve into milestones, and these milestones mark events that are so powerful and so transformative that the history of our very community is rewritten. I now officially open the first commencement exercises and officially welcome the first graduating class of the school, the seniors of 2013!" Then the former first lady of the United States of America, Laura Bush, spoke: "In four short years, Cristo Rey Jesuit has come so far, so fast, as you have taken the city by storm!" And our keynote speaker and Cristo Rey Jesuit supporter, successful Houston businessman Richard Kinder, added this important point: "In this area of Houston, a feasibility study reported a close to 60 percent—get that number, 60 percent—dropout rate among sophomores in high school. But because of Cristo Rey Jesuit's outstanding program, your brave move to join it, and the hard work everybody has done to see it through, you don't have a 60 percent dropout rate. In fact, every senior at Cristo Rey Jesuit has been accepted to college, and that deserves a big round of applause."

Transformative indeed! Life changing! But you must *want* it. As you know, it is not an easy road at Cristo Rey Jesuit, especially with the demanding academic work and the corporate work-study program. And I know that the focus from the beginning to get into college can seem overwhelming! But it can lead you to a better life in many possible ways: greater wealth, more security, better health, closer family, and stronger community.

The facts don't lie: without a high school education, your options are severely limited. So, by earning a diploma at Cristo Rey Jesuit, you have already taken a very important step. And then there is college.

College can add many more options for a better life, and the statistics prove the point. College graduates earn an average of $22,000 per year more than people with only a high school diploma. This not only means you might be able to afford to buy more things you need, but it gives you and your family better security—the security to support your loved ones, the security to be independent, and with less worry. College graduates are about half as likely to be unemployed, and more likely to have jobs that provide health care. College will give you broader experiences in the world, and thus you will be more likely to bring a taste of that back to your family and inspire the next generation to achieve even more than you. As college graduates, statistics show that you will be much more likely to read to your children and take them to cultural events, thus broadening their horizons and instilling closer family ties. And college helps you build a better *community*, as you learn about societal problems and how to collaborate with others to solve them.

Are you convinced yet? Let me put it another way: You got into Cristo Rey Jesuit because you are smart and motivated to learn. But you also *had* to be "underprivileged"—a nice way of saying "poor," or from a challenging socioeconomic position. I know you hate the description, and in many ways, don't even feel it. But it's a fact, and it's not your fault, just like the fact that I am short. It's just where we find you today. Again, statistics tell the story: without a college degree, you have only a 14 percent chance of getting into the top socioeconomic class, and a 45 percent chance of staying where you are. With a college degree, your chance of getting to the top increases to 40 percent—about three times better, and only a 16 percent chance of staying where you are.

How do I know all this? People who care about *you* send me the results of studies done on this and related topics, and I use that information to show people in the broader Houston community *why* they should help support our efforts at Cristo Rey Jesuit. Now I am sharing it with you to show the dramatic change a college degree can make in your lives: it can be transformative!

But I would be kidding you if I said it would be *easy*. It's not easy. At Cristo Rey, we bring you into a new world— one where you help earn an education that you cannot otherwise afford, one where you rub shoulders in your jobs with the kind of professionals you may aspire to become. We try to make it a safe environment for you, and we are here to provide daily guidance.

But college is a different deal altogether. We cannot be there with you, though we pledge to try to keep an eye on you from a distance! We want you to succeed in college, just as you did in Cristo Rey Jesuit, so here are some tips to consider that we have learned from those who went before you.

First, you will be in the minority economically. Most college kids will have lots of extra money to spend and you won't. Don't worry about it. You are as good as they are and maybe even better prepared for life, because you know what it means to be without all the things you want. Your poverty is *real*, but it's nothing to be ashamed of. Your job, and our objective together, is to improve the situation!

The statistics suggest that, even though you are as academically qualified, because you come from a lower socio-economic class, your probability of graduating from college is much less than those students with rich parents. The numbers say your chances are about *half* as good, unless you keep in mind some of the things I am going to tell you now. There are many, many reasons for this—none relating to your intelligence—but you, my young friends, have been down this road before, and defied the same odds at Cristo Rey Jesuit. Indeed, with the weight of poverty pulling you down, you have successfully defied gravity! *And you can do it again in college!*

A study done at the University of Texas in the last couple of years and reported by Paul Tough on May 15, 2014, in the *New York Times Magazine* article "Who Gets to

Graduate?" noted the following: "Every college freshman— rich or poor, white or minority, first generation or legacy— experiences academic setbacks and awkward moments when they feel they don't belong."

The study found that students who are in a minority position—whether by race or socioeconomic class—often misinterpret these *temporary* setbacks as a *permanent* indication that they can't succeed in college. You'll be riding high from your high school success at Cristo Rey Jesuit, and then an early failure in college can erode your confidence and raise doubts in your mind about belonging and ability. If unchecked, these doubts can grow and create "a sense of helplessness" that may lead to a "self-fulfilling prophecy" of defeat.

Do not let this happen to you! I have seen you in the hallway at school, and I have talked to you, and I *know* you are convinced that a college education is in your future. After all, that's the focus of our school: "*College* Preparatory!" And you *will* be ready.

Second, focus on what matters: studying, learning, and making the grades. There was no substitute for this at Cristo Rey Jesuit, and the same holds true in college. After college, you will want a job in the field of your choice. And the best jobs go to those who make the grades.

What happens when you *fail* at getting good grades? It might happen at first. It happened to me, in fact, and almost everyone has a similar bad experience. College is a step up in academic rigor from high school, even from Cristo Rey Jesuit. You will need to get used to the new *intensity*, the new *speed* with which material must be mastered, and maybe a new way to study. But you wouldn't be in college if you couldn't do it. Lots of smart people thought so too, as they reviewed your application. So, look at a bad grade as an opportunity, a chance to figure it out with the help of your professor, your friends, and your study group. It's just a speed bump. And never forget that in college you are part of a "community of high-achieving scholars"—and you *belong* there.

Third, don't be afraid to ask for help. I did that when I went to college. The transition from Brownsville, Texas, to Boston College was a huge step for me culturally, and I didn't fit in right away. As I tried to adjust to my new life in college, I called on my teachers back in Texas and my family, if only to share my doubts and fears, and get a little pep talk. It always helped! And don't forget your new teachers in college. Most are decent folks who will want to see you succeed and will be flattered that you stopped by to see them. And maybe most important in your "support group" are your classmates from Cristo Rey Jesuit. Stay in contact with them! They know you, they know where you came from, and they are going through the same adjustment issues as you.

Next, try to find a few *new* good friends to hang out with, to study or eat with, or be in a club with. When I first got to college, I felt left out of things, but then I discovered that *everyone* felt this way. And maybe for you, coming from a different socioeconomic class from many of the students in your college, you *may* feel more isolated at first. Take some risks and step out of your comfort zone to engage new people. This will likely be the *hardest* part of your transition, because it will feel like you are separating yourself from your old life, and maybe not giving your old friends and family the attention that you (or for that matter, they) think they deserve. But this is just another part of your "education"—learning to exist in *both* worlds. College is your new "neighborhood," so get a few close buddies who will be there for you. Pick them carefully, as they will likely become lifelong friends, or even people with whom you will work in the future. Remember the fate of Francis Xavier after he met Ignatius of Loyola at college in Paris; it changed the course of his life, and of the world!

Even though I have given you the *economic* incentives of a college education, remember that it is more than these. It's about creating options and finding what is best for you, what you are passionate about. Find *this* and you will be happier, and the rest will take care of itself, including your ability to make the world a better place.

In searching for your passion in life, I offer one small piece of advice, which I must have said a million times: *never forget to dream big!*

Finally, education doesn't end with college. Once you start down this path, you will be learning new things for the rest of your life. Just as you did with your corporate work-study program in high school, your job *after* college will be a constant learning experience. If you land a job you really like, it will be fun; if not, do it well, but be searching for that next opportunity.

There is no shame if the career you thought you would like doesn't work out, or if your interests simply change. This happened to me when I decided to become a Jesuit priest after completing a law degree! However, changing career paths may require some retooling. Remember the life of St. Ignatius, who spent the first thirty years of his life preparing for and being a professional soldier—a Spanish knight. Then he had a change of heart, and spent the next nineteen years of his life—from the time he was injured in battle in 1521 to 1540—discovering his new calling, reeducating himself, and forming the Jesuit order. He literally went back to school in his thirties—can you imagine? When he died at age sixty-five, on July 31, 1556, he had devoted only sixteen years to being the head of the new

Jesuit order. But it was the work that earned him an eternal place in history—and more.

Had Ignatius remained a soldier, certainly *our* lives today would be different. Perhaps he would have been killed in battle later in his life, or retired to live as a nobleman in Spain. We would probably have never known of him. Certainly, there would have been no Jesuit Order as we know it today, and perhaps no Cristo Rey Jesuit College Preparatory School in Houston, Texas! Yet each part of the life of Ignatius was critical to the success of the next phase of his life: a foundation of military leadership and prowess led to a search for a more meaningful endeavor and additional education, which ultimately positioned him to lead a new religious order. Indeed, the largest religious order in the Roman Catholic Church.

It will be the same for you. Your high school education is the foundation for college, which becomes the foundation for your career, which becomes the foundation for the good you will do in this world. Every phase *must* be done with excellence to support the next. I know it will take much hard work and determination on your part, but trust me that it is worth the effort. I likely won't be around to tell you in person, "I told you so!" But trust me on this—it will be so!

Building a better life for yourself and your family may seem like a long journey. But as our Chinese friend Lao-tzu said 2,700 years ago, "A journey of a thousand miles begins with a single step." Getting a quality high school education is only the first step of that journey. Take the journey one step at a time, and remember to enjoy the moment you are in: high school, college, and then a job. Find your passion, and learn all you can to pursue it. The rest will work out.

PART III

YOU WILL FIND A WAY!

Do the difficult now, and the impossible soon thereafter.

—Father T.J. Martinez, SJ

6

SET THE WORLD ON FIRE

"Excellence is not expected in this family...it is *required*." This was the "prime directive" that my dad gave us growing up in the family, and the words still ring loudly in my ears after all these years. Wow! What a standard to live up to! And I know we four children did not always succeed. But we always tried hard in whatever we attempted, and looking back, I think my sister did the best!

At Cristo Rey Jesuit, we are a family, too. You are the highlight of my life, and when you call me "*Father* Martinez," I know it's a "title" for a priest, but with you I see it more broadly. I care about you—*I love you*—and like any loving parent, I want to see you succeed in life and be happy, productive, caring people. We are a family!

This is the core chapter of the book and, unfortunately, the longest. But it's stuff you need—or will need—in the future. I hope you will have others in your life that will share similar advice with you, but just in case you run short, you'll always have me!

First, and most importantly, I want you to know that I *trust* you. By high school, you are young adults, and most of you are mature beyond your years. But the world is a complex place, so some guidance might be in order, just a little, to help you along your way. I am not talking about religious guidance—though that's important too—and we will have an opportunity to discuss that later. Rather, let's focus now on some practical guidance, the kind you might get from a parent, a teacher, a mentor, a friend, or even a priest!

My dad demanded excellence from us, and even though it seemed hard to accomplish, we *always* tried. In fact, as kids we were a little afraid to object! But we came to understand that he demanded it because he loved us, and dad knew we needed always to give our best effort to succeed in an increasingly complex and competitive world. So, I am going to say the same to you: *excellence is required!*

Dad meant it to apply to all aspects of our lives, and so do I. Education was surely a key part of that. He knew that, for his kids to have a chance in this world, a quality education was a requirement—and that it had to be completed with excellence. But we have already discussed that issue.

Now I want to speak about a few other important aspects of your life, things we would have discussed in a longer life together. And all of which will make excellence a part of your life. Read them one at a time, all together, or in any order; it doesn't matter. But please consider them carefully, as I have.

BEING GRATEFUL

Be thankful for what you have in this life, no matter how little it may be. Living with an "attitude of gratitude" is one of the most important lessons I can leave you with. It is why you hear it from me so often! I promise you: by keeping your focus on gratitude you will be a happier, healthier, and more successful person.

St. Ignatius said this about gratitude in a letter he wrote in 1542:

> It seems to me…that ingratitude is one of the things most worthy of detestation before our Creator and Lord…for it is a failure to recognize the good things, the graces, and gifts received. As such, it is the cause, beginning, and origin of all evils and sins. On the contrary, recognition and gratitude for the good things and gifts received is greatly loved and esteemed both in heaven and on earth.

This is as true today as it was in the time of St. Ignatius. I believe it, and I can "preach it" supported by the Scriptures. But it's also just good common sense.

Gratitude as a basic attitude of life means being thankful on a daily basis for the things you receive and for the "giver" of those things. It is more than merely expressing thanks—though *that* is important too—it is making a life of gratitude the goal: being *good* to each other, living a life of self-control and perseverance, and focusing on what life has given you, rather than on what you think you *deserve* from life.

Maybe all this sounds obvious, but it's not an easy thing to do. To help us in our life as Jesuit priests, St. Ignatius gave us the daily *Examen* Prayer, the first part of which is gratitude: to recall the gifts we have received from God that day and to give thanks for them. It's a useful exercise that anyone can do, and it can be broadened to remember the gifts received from others. Being thankful in this way allows you to remember the positive things and people in your lives, and that allows you to live a life focused on happiness and success: to exercise self-control in your actions in order to avoid the many pitfalls and temptations in life that will get you off track; to work hard to achieve your goals in life and persevere against the obstacles that will come to block your way; and, finally, to be patient with others, and forgive them if they cause you trouble or harm. Okay, I know! These are very hard things to do!

Here are some examples of what I mean. You might say, "I am unlucky because I come from a broken home," or "I have only one parent." But in living the "attitude of gratitude" you could instead rejoice in the people you *do* have around you who love you, and care for you, and focus on *those* relationships. For example, I might say, "Why was I hit with this cancer?" But then I realize how going through this has brought me closer to family and friends, and has showed me how full my life is with you all in it!

Today, there is plenty we could complain about, especially for young people: the economy is a mess and getting a good job, or any job, is a challenge; competition is stiffer and there is huge pressure to do well academically; there's much confusion about sex and sexual identity; and then there are threats to personal safety in an increasingly violent world, which is a constant concern. These are just the *big* things that we all talk about every day. Sometimes the future looks rather bleak, indeed! But self-pity and complaining only holds you back in life, and the negative attitude blinds you to the potential *good* things you already have that can improve your life, and the lives of all those around you.

I know you *already* get the idea. You might have said many times, "I am poor, what do I have to be thankful for?" But I have never heard you complain because you have already figured out that you have the gift of life—and with that the means to make your life better.

A positive attitude—an attitude of gratitude—will help create happiness in your life, where you may have thought there could be none. And that will lead to a healthier life. It's not just a spiritual thing, but also a scientific fact, because your mind is a powerful thing. Try it, and you'll see!

FOLLOWING YOUR DREAMS

Questions I hear all the time from students in high school are, "What am I going to do with my life? What am I going to be? How do I know if I am following the right path?" These are important questions and hard to answer. Trust me when I tell you many others of all ages have the same questions: college students often change their majors and career path, college graduates often reevaluate the same questions after they start their first full-time job, and even older people question the path they are on!

I struggled to figure out my *true* calling, and bounced around along the way quite a bit: Boston College under-graduate degree in political science, volunteer work in New York City, a law degree from the University of Texas, and finally, at age twenty-six, I joined the Society of Jesus. I was *finally* following my dream, but it even took a few more years of chasing it: theology at Weston, a master's in education at Harvard, and lots of additional training. It can take time to discover your dream, and then more time to attain it, so be patient—but *keep asking questions*!

There is no shame in changing your mind; many people do. I did! It may turn out that you need to try several different things before you find what really fits you. But, provided you undertake quality opportunities—no matter what they are—with each step along the way, you will learn things that will help you in your next endeavor. It is never a waste of time to follow your heart and mind to interesting educational or work experiences, even if the "end game" is still a bit unclear. It's okay to take some risks; taking a risk for a good cause will never turn out to be a bad thing.

After consulting your own heart and your own mind, also listen to others who care about you. They may have ideas you haven't thought about: your parents, your teachers, your counselors and mentors, and maybe even me! And don't neglect to listen to your friends, and hear their ideas, their own goals and aspirations.

I have been walking the halls of Cristo Rey Jesuit for almost six years, and have listened to you talk about your dreams—each an individual dream, each a special story in the making. I know you all by name, I know your stories, and I was always so thrilled to hear your plans. Here are just a few:

> *My dream is to graduate from college.*
>
> *I want to be a heart surgeon.*
>
> *I want to design computer software.*
>
> *When I grow up, I want to be a CEO of a major performing arts company.*
>
> *I want to be something big.*
>
> *I want to study psychology, and then be a chef.*
>
> *I want to be a professional soccer player…or a forensic scientist.*
>
> *My dream is to be an engineer.*
>
> *I want to operate a shoe company business—everybody likes shoes.*
>
> *My dream is to become a successful black woman, take care of my family and friends, and keep in touch with them, and to care for my grandma.*
>
> *I want to be able to change this world.*
>
> *I'm not sure I know what I want to be yet, but I know I want to help other people.*
>
> *I want to be a Father.…I'll have a family, and take care of my family…and I'll have Father Martinez in my house…and I'll build a chapel.*
>
> *My dream is to help children in the inner cities with their struggles, because they have one parent…and I know how that feels.*
>
> *In the future, I picture myself being very successful,*

raising a family—a happy family—and looking back to this school and saying, I came here and they helped me be where I am.

I want to go to college at NYU....I want to go to Baylor University....I want to go to Texas....We are living that dream now at Cristo Rey....I never dreamed a school could be like this.

These are all worthy dreams, and they, and even more, are attainable by you. Though you may change them as you get more education and experiences in life, never forget to dream big. You're worth it, and you can do it!

HAVING NO UPPER LIMIT

The first president at Rice University here in Houston challenged the university "to assign no upper limit to our educational endeavor." A couple of years ago, I participated in their graduation ceremony, and just by looking at the students, you can see that Rice is full of smart kids. While it's probably true that most of their students started with many advantages that you don't have, they are *no* smarter! And you are motivated in ways many of them cannot yet appreciate. That's why I *know* that you have no upper limit.

Many of you have extra challenges in your life. Some of you have been thrust into adult roles at home way too early. Many of your families have only one parent in the household. Some of you live below the poverty level to such an extent that when we ask you—as we do everyone—to contribute what you can toward your education, you are like one mother of the first graduating class who could only afford to pay in tortillas. Of course, I gladly accepted because they were great tortillas!

Many of you will be the first to ever graduate from high school in your family, and many of you never thought that college was even a possibility in your life. Certainly, you have different backgrounds and fewer privileges than many college students today, but you are not alone and you do have some distinct advantages: you are highly motivated; you have the support of all of us at Cristo Rey Jesuit; and, we are smart too! We know your capabilities, and we *know* you can do it. That's why we tell you that you can succeed from day one. Cristo Rey Jesuit is a revolution in education in Houston. It's a game changer, and you are part of it; in fact, you are the reason the game is changing!

The mission of our school is to unleash the potential hidden in the children of the most economically deprived part of Houston. While you are pulled down by many circumstances over which you have never had control, you consistently defy gravity and achieve your dreams. I remember when Elizabeth Martinez (great name, but no relation) got her college acceptance. She told me, "I got accepted to my top school, my top choice. Who would have ever thought that the girl from the *barrio* is going to an out-of-state college?" And another of your classmates almost broke my heart when his freshman grades put him on the borderline of getting dismissed from Cristo Rey Jesuit. I told him I loved him and that I expected a lot from him, but that I was very disappointed because I knew that he could do much better. In fact, I was totally frustrated and a bit angry inside, though I tried hard not to show it, because I suspected family issues at home were at least part of the problem for his lack of focus. Even so, I was relentless in bugging him about getting his work done, and then in an amazing way, something clicked: he took *seven* courses in summer school to make up his work, and is now attending the University of Houston. Defying gravity—it's a beautiful thing to see!

Sometimes all it takes to unlock the potential in each of you is to know that we believe in you; that alone can be transformative. I've seen it in myself, too. I remember when I was assigned here to Cristo Rey Jesuit that I had doubts, and even expressed it to some people I already knew in Houston: "I am too young to run a school!" "I know I can relate to kids, but I don't have any business sense!" And the big concern: "I don't know how to raise money!" But my Jesuit superiors believed in me, the initial committee and board of trustees believed in me, and working hard *together*, we made it work.

At Cristo Rey Jesuit, we are all thrilled to be here in school with you. We want the best for you. This program and your hard work saves lives—and families. The transformation we have seen in you is that *you* realize that quickly, too! You begin to believe that, indeed, *you can do it!*

At graduation, one of your classmates put it to me this way: "Anything is possible now, anything can happen." I just hugged him and smiled, and thought to myself, "They get it!"

BEING A GOOD LEADER

Men and women of character are built with constraint, with humility, and with a focus on living a life for others. True leadership is done more by example than by authority: it's *how* you live your life, your values, and your loyalty and commitment to the endeavor at hand. Being a good leader is mostly about *who* you are. What you do is important, but without a solid values-based foundation, you will never reach your full potential as a leader.

Being a good leader starts with being a good *follower*—by learning from the experience of others, and then *listening* carefully to their desires and ideas. Listening is hard, but if done properly it will yield fantastic results, because by listening to others at a deep level, you learn their motivations, values, and desires. Knowing what others want in life as well as their life experiences and expertise is invaluable to guiding people successfully to a common objective. You can't get that by dictating, ordering people around, or by stubbornly imposing your own ideas on others. It simply won't work. Instead, with each person you meet, treat them as if they are the most important person in the world, and then listen to their passions and to their heart.

Good leadership also requires *sharing*—share your information, your ideas, your passions. In doing so, you will educate others about things they may not have considered, and in turn, they will be more motivated to share their thoughts. But do it with humility, remembering always that humility is the quickest way to earn respect.

A good leader is *positive*—people respond openly to a positive attitude and an appropriate sense of humor. Good leaders make others feel comfortable in a constantly changing world, and bring a laugh when people need a laugh. This may be especially appropriate when you encounter failure. Look for the good in failures, the lessons learned. Find peace in them and use them to motivate people to a higher level of achievement.

A good leader will also focus on the best qualities of each person...and you will find that by not putting other people down, you will automatically lift yourself up as a leader. It is human nature: you unlock the best potential in the people around you when they know they have your trust, value, and respect.

Finally, always *challenge* yourself. Only by carefully examining what you want, and constantly reexamining it, will you be able to inspire *others* to follow your vision.

Challenging yourself allows you to sharpen your own vision, and at the same time stay open to adapting to new opportunities—they always come along.

HAVING RESPONSIBILITY

Your school motto—*Magis*—meaning "more" or "greater" in Latin, imposes obligations on each of you. There is a responsibility that comes with the opportunities you have been given. In fact, we all have this duty to strive for the *magis*—to seek to do more and to reach for unimagined heights, whether we are a student at Cristo Rey Jesuit or not. I am confident that you will discover, as I have, that it's not really the "burden" it might seem at first, because this duty, this obligation, this responsibility has its own reward: true happiness comes in serving others.

First, as students and young adults, is your responsibility to yourselves and to your immediate family. Strive to achieve to your best abilities, to exercise self-control, to always do the right thing, and to accomplish the mission of being as well educated as possible: first, your high school diploma; next, a good college education; and then, a job you enjoy.

Second, you can focus on your broader family here at Cristo Rey Jesuit College Prep: your teachers, administrators, the other students, and, of course, me! As a family, we are obliged—even honored—to support each other, and in giving to others, you will receive even more in return in a life well-lived.

You have God-given gifts: talents, opportunities, and personality traits that allow you to connect in your own unique way with people. Perhaps you bring a good sense of humor, a positive attitude about life, or an ability to empathize with others. One of your obligations in life is to figure out how to use these gifts to their full potential—first in achieving your own potential, and then as a role model on display for others to follow. It has been a delight to see that you are already doing this, and that many are following your example: brothers, sisters, cousins, and neighbors. Your efforts are transforming your lives as well as the lives of those around you.

Once you have worked hard to help yourself and those close to you, you can strive for the *magis* again in doing more to help others whom you don't even know: to open the doors to the same opportunities you had, to not only show them the way, but also to pave the way for them. In doing so, you will be changing the world for the better at an increasingly rapid rate—from just one of you, many will follow. That's truly transformative!

My dream is that eventually you will move beyond being just role models for the students that follow in your footsteps, and become the new supporters and leaders— business owners, employers, leaders in the community, the corporate sponsors of future work-study programs, and donors to the school. Yes! As hard as that might be for you to imagine today, my dream is that you will someday do that—and more.

These responsibilities, these obligations, are not only the right thing for you to do, they will also give you true happiness in serving others as you will be living life to the fullest!

FINDING A WAY

No matter how bad you think you have it, there is always someone else who is worse off. I never cease to be amazed that, in the human struggle for success, for happiness, for a meaningful and full life, even in the worst of circumstances, people can find a way to a better life.

Last year, my Jesuit superiors called me to take a leave of absence from Cristo Rey Jesuit to undertake a six-month mission in Kenya in preparation for my final vows. I saw first-hand a confluence of faith and destitution that I had never witnessed before, with living conditions, including roaming packs of wild dogs, animals that at night made bloodcurdling screams, and squadrons of mosquitos bombarding the netting around my sleeping mat, that made my Jesuit community accommodations in Houston seem like a five-star resort. Add to this the daily 4 a.m. Muslim call to prayer blasting from speakers, and you get the idea: this certainly wasn't Texas!

On a deeper level, this privileged opportunity to be a Jesuit missionary was quite powerful and moving. The Kenyan Jesuits are very simple and live very austerely. They are young and numerous and fun-loving, and very much on fire with God. Amidst desperate poverty, they are full of faith and hope.

Among my most moving experiences was a visit to a congregation in the middle of the largest and most dangerous slum in Nairobi called Kibera. I was asked to say Mass for a Catholic community at a "missionary outpost church," which required that I be dropped off right in the center of the slum and continue the journey on foot. The outpost mission was called "Christ the King"—literally Cristo Rey—so I knew instantly that I was destined to go, but I was on my own!

Approaching the depths of the slum, I could see rows and rows of rusted corrugated metal and rotting cardboard boxes, leaning against each other almost haphazardly. What I initially took for a dumping area soon revealed itself to be a chaos of ramshackle and ragged shanty hovels, each one housing entire families, with kids running around trying to sell old shoes, used cans of Raid mosquito spray, and day old bread brought back to life by frying it in used animal fat. As I slowly wound my way through the red, cratered, unpaved mud roads that crisscrossed the slums, I couldn't help but see inside: some family members were sleeping, others cooking over slow-burning fires, and the rest tumbling through the door openings in front and out on to the dirt roads. They saw me too, a lone Tex-Mex priest awash in an ocean of Africans living in a literal jungle of debilitating and oppressive poverty and pain. I was nervous.

Then I spied something interesting that momentarily distracted my attention from the uncomfortable surroundings. On top of each of these "shacks" was yet a higher-level landscape populated with antennas, each made from a long piece of wire and a steel pole, with a dish on top. Those poles ran downward right into the center of these one-room "homes" and connected to a small television that sat in the middle of the dirt-floored room, becoming an electronic hearth for the family. They displayed the familiar blue-white glow that I could see through cutouts in the cardboard walls, with the audio of familiar American sitcoms. It was surreal: *Two and a Half Men*—one of their favorite shows—blaring on these old TVs among the crush of people, the visual poverty, the dirt-caked kids, and the rocky, waterlogged, uneven dirt alleys.

I remember asking myself, "How in the world did they get electricity into a place like this?" Later, my Jesuit superior offered a simple answer: "They find a way."

This was a level of desperate poverty that I had only seen in films or heard about from other missionary priests. My expectations for the Mass I was heading to became lower and lower; after all, I thought, "Who in the world, amid this seemingly hopeless striving for survival, would make time for Mass?" After walking for about half an hour, and winding my way through the chaos and madness of the slum, I came upon a larger version of the metal and cardboard molehills I had just seen with a sign on it that simply said, "Chapel." I was relieved to find the place, but also wondered, embarrassingly, how anyone could find Christ in such chaotic, desperate, and even dangerous surroundings.

But God never ceases to surprise me. In the midst of this seeping squalor stood a massive throng of Kenyan men, women, and children, dressed elegantly and colorfully, and singing, clapping, and dancing. All of whom were ready—if not starving—for a good word and the good Lord. My heart nearly exploded with jubilance at this magnificent sight in total contrast to the depraved reality that I had just walked through. The hope, the optimism, the faith, the joy, the celebration, the love, the family, the reverence, the devotion, the unabashed praise of God—all overwhelming, and if I had died at that very moment, I would have died in pure revelry, as it felt like I had crossed a threshold from tragic despair into the promised land—a threshold that took me from hell straight into heaven!

With one person holding a candle so I could put on my vestments, and then flanked by *ten* young altar servers and *twenty* eucharistic ministers, we paraded in front of the altar in this "shed church" to thunderous applause. One young fellow held an electric lightbulb connected to a long cord as a "spotlight" on the sanctuary, while another handed me a microphone. Again, I asked myself, "Where in the world did they get the electricity?" But then I totally soaked in their raw exhilaration and faith-filled festive fire and responded in kind with my own ear-to-ear smile and simply began, "In the name of the Father...."

Yes, you may start with certain disadvantages in your life. And yes, there may be obstacles in your path—and most certainly, writing your own story and achieving your dreams won't be easy. But I am certain that you too will find a way!

LETTING GO

Like your parents, I will never be ready to let you go. But for you to succeed in this complex world, I *must* do that, and someday you will find yourself in the same position with respect to those you mentor. You must learn to navigate your future path independently, and I know you can. I trust you and will *always* be with you in spirit.

It was the same for the school. I was not ready this year to let go of Cristo Rey Jesuit of Houston, but I knew I would eventually have to do that. My illness forced my hand: first, on what I had hoped would be temporary, and later, on a permanent basis.

Indeed, God has his own way of telling us when to let go. I trust you, the students, and your hard working teachers and administrators, to be good shepherds of what we have built together. And again, know that I will always be with you in spirit.

St. Ignatius knew what "letting go" required, and knew just what to say to his missionary priests and students that he sent out to make a better world: *ite, inflammate omnia*.

And so, I now say it to you: "Go forth and set the world on fire!"

7
EVERYONE IS SPECIAL

Ironically, the endoscopy procedure that would confirm my cancer diagnosis—among the worst news I ever received in my life—also reminded me of how every person I meet is so very special.

After returning from my six-month mission to Africa in December 2013, I knew something was wrong. My stomach was unsettled, but I figured it was something I had eaten in Africa. Believe me, there were a lot of "unknowns" on my plate, but I ate what they ate. So initially, I ignored the discomfort.

Integrating back into life in Cristo Rey Jesuit and Houston was a whirlwind of activity, and then some wonderful supporters and close friends invited me to join them for a few days in Rome, where I said Mass in the rooms once occupied by St. Ignatius next to the Church of the Gesù—the home church for the Jesuit order. What a wonderful once-in-a-lifetime experience!

Once back in Houston, life resumed at high speed, but still I didn't feel quite right and my appetite had certainly not returned to normal. Even my favorite Whataburger hamburgers didn't tempt me as in the past. I thought it might still be bacteria from food in Africa and had some treatment for that, but the problem persisted.

Then in March the following year, the pain suddenly got worse to the point that I went to the hospital, where they did an endoscopy—a procedure in which you are anesthetized and a small camera is run inside to take a closer look at the stomach. They also took a sample of tissue. All very standard procedures, but new to me. So, I was a bit nervous.

That's when I met the nurses and technicians. What a wonderful, dedicated group of people. Even though my procedure was very minor (ten minutes after they put me to sleep) and even though there were scores of other patients—many getting much more complicated and serious procedures—these nurses and technicians made me feel special, as though I was the only one in the room, as though I was the only medical procedure on the schedule for that day.

They did it without me even noticing, never bringing attention to themselves. They let me talk—and you know how I love to talk! So, they quickly learned about my passion for the Jesuit order, and my passion for Cristo Rey Jesuit College Prep. They were also open and friendly about themselves too when I asked about their families and their interests in life. Soon, I was asleep with a smile on my face. And the procedure was over! Simple!

When Mom and my brother Trey found me in the recovery room some thirty minutes later, I woke up relieved, feeling no pain from the procedure. Still in a bit of the anesthesia twilight, I instantly and quite loudly, I am told, awarded all the nurses and technicians an A+, not because the procedure had gone so well—which of course it had—but because they had made me smile and feel like I was the most special person in the room.

We all possess the ability to make others feel special, but we often miss the opportunities to do it. Here in the hospital, with my own private concerns, I was reminded of something far more important: *everyone is special.*

Each of you is a special gift of life: unique, with potential beyond imagination, and with many talents. Of course, not everyone is good at everything. I am awful at math! But that's not really the point. The point is that if you take the time to really learn about a person, you will find a special talent in everyone. In the process, you will give them the gift of your full and undivided attention and you may make them feel like they are the most special person in the room.

When I recovered more fully from the anesthesia after the endoscopy, I could introduce all the nurses and technicians to my mom and my brother. And I didn't hold anything back when I said they were the best nurses and technicians in the building: best at what they do (I survived the procedure!), best looking, and smartest. And though I didn't say this aloud, best at making me feel special when I most needed it. Everyone got an A+.

Everybody has an A+ within them waiting to be discovered. I believe this to my core. And when I look hard for the goodness in each person I meet, I am never disappointed. It brings joy at no cost, and unlocks goodness and potential. St. Ignatius teaches us to look hard to find God in everything: we are all gifts of God, and each of us is unique and in some way the most special person in the room!

8
WHO IS YOUR HERO?

Everybody needs a hero. However, picking a hero requires some care and thought. You want to get it right, and you don't want to leave anybody out. Really, maybe it's wise to have more than one. So, here are some ideas!

A hero might be somebody that inspires you—perhaps somebody you place on a pedestal and aspire to follow. It could be an individual or a group of individuals you particularly admire, like firefighters or people in the military or teachers. Maybe you know them or maybe not. A hero can be a famous historical figure that you want to pattern your life after, or someone living that you may interact with in this lifetime. It could even be a parent, brother, sister, or other relative. How many times have we thought that our mom or our dad was our hero? Many times, over the years, I'll bet!

True heroes demonstrate grace and courage in their actions, and treat others with generosity and kindness regardless of social status, income level, or the number of world-beating accomplishments on their résumé. A hero is one who has a positive impact on your life, and even the seemingly small things matter!

It's possible that your heroes will change over time as you mature and gain more life experiences. Maybe those in your past who didn't seem to fit the role when you knew them suddenly reveal themselves to be of "hero caliber." Whoever they are, pick your heroes carefully, because your heroes reflect who you are!

For me, most of the people I put on a pedestal are the ones who do two things: they call me out of a group of people as being very special, and then they push me, or "stretch me," to take who I am and what I can offer to the next level.

Many of these people have been my teachers at various stages, so I'll tell you about just a few now, and disclose others later when I tell you a little about my life before Cristo Rey Jesuit. I have other heroes, too, who were never in the role of a formal teacher, but nevertheless taught me a great deal by the way they lived their lives. So, while there are many, here are just a few who have helped shape my life:

> *Professor Charles Alan Wright* was my constitutional law and federal courts teacher at the University of Texas Law School, and a living legend. I was afraid of him at first and worried that my GPA would suffer, but he just kept calling on me during class to answer question after question. That made me "stretch," for I had to prepare thoroughly or risk looking foolish. After the courses were over, he and I continued our friendship for many years and shared a love of the history and philosophy of the law.
>
> *Tom Clancy, SJ*, taught me Jesuit history in my novitiate stage of formation. He made it come alive for me. He was such a great teacher, and I hope all of you have at least one like him. He made St. Ignatius a living and relevant person for me in today's world, and on the long road of Jesuit formation, inspired me and many others to keep to our vows, our work, and our studies.

I am very proud to be a Jesuit, and proud to be a Jesuit brother of such a teacher.

Dr. Ardis Collins was my professor in modern philosophy following the novitiate during my Jesuit formation in the "First Studies" program at Loyola University in Chicago. I had just proclaimed my initial vows of poverty, obedience, and chastity, and this was the first "deep dive" into the formal educational requirements of the Jesuit order. I really wanted to do well. She was very demanding, and I had observed that she demanded the most only from those she thought were brilliant. Imagine my pleasure when she pulled me aside and encouraged me to do a research philosophy master's degree on top of the Jesuit requirements! She then mentored me on my thesis on Hegel, for which I was given an award of distinction that automatically reserved a spot for me for doctoral studies in philosophy should I want to return later. She was demanding, she pushed me hard, and I loved it!

Mr. Mike Earsing was principal, and now president, at Dallas Jesuit College Prep. He took me under his wing and taught me how to navigate being a "high school Jesuit"—he really showed me how it all worked. After my first year, he promoted me to director of the Community Service & Social Justice Program, and asked me to "stretch" beyond the normal three-year teaching assignment to try out administration, and at the same time revamp the program to make it an exciting, mission-oriented endeavor, one that had more impact for the greater Dallas community. What a great opportunity and yet another building block for my future work at Cristo Rey Jesuit!

Dr. Mary Grassa O'Neil was one of my professors at Harvard who searched me out after she had read my admittance application, and encouraged me to move from one program to a higher grad school program she oversaw—again, another "stretch move." She taught me bold leadership and how to incorporate the latest research into a Catholic high school culture. The wink she gave me just as I started my graduation speech was a priceless award for me: her unspoken vote of confidence. What perfect timing for her to come into my life!

Archbishop Joseph A. Fiorenza has been a fine example during my six years at Cristo Rey Jesuit. A man who could have simply said, "I'm retired, and don't need to be a tireless supporter," has instead been outspoken and actively with us all the way. He could have easily justified sitting on the sidelines and not taken another risk in his life; after all, he had marched for racial justice with Martin Luther King in Selma, Alabama—wouldn't that have been enough? But he jumped in and joined our team in building Cristo Rey Jesuit of Houston, and energized us all in the process. And always, he did it with grace, humility, and good humor. He is truly a hero for all of us!

After coming to Houston to help found Cristo Rey Jesuit, I found many more heroes: people to admire, people who were generous with their time and talent, people who had a huge impact on my life—supporters, donors, engaged board members, tireless and talented teachers and staff, and of course you students!

Finally, during these last few months while fighting this cancer, my family have been my superheroes with their care, their time commitment, their questioning and discussion, and ultimately their understanding and acceptance of me. All this has helped me face the facts of my life better, and has "stretched me" in how I conduct my life, because I would never want to disappoint them.

It's important to have a hero or two in your back pocket, at least as a role model to help you focus on how you want to live and to function in your life. Pick your heroes carefully, cherish their example and advice, and try to exceed even what they did. That's what true heroes would want!

PART IV

THE MAN YOU WOULD HAVE KNOWN

Over a lifetime, we would have become close friends, and you all would have come to know all 5' 5" of "this little Jesuit."

—Father T.J. Martinez, SJ

9
FINDING THE
RIGHT PATH

It might be easy for you to think, "Father Martinez doesn't really understand where I come from, so why should I listen to his advice?" So, maybe given a snapshot of my background, you will perhaps see some similarities with your upbringing.

There are not many places in the United States of America farther south than Brownsville, Texas. In fact, it is just barely in America—geographically and culturally, it's almost Mexico. Nobody really comes to Brownsville, unless they need to. There are no national parks to visit, no world-renowned museums, no professional sports teams, no world-class theater. And the elements are awful: hot, humid, dusty, and flat, with the occasional hurricane to flush it clean.

However, Brownsville was the center of *my* world. It was where I learned right from wrong, where I got my educational foundation, and where I was raised to be the man I am today by what I call my "all-American family," with all the good and bad that term implies. I would recommend Brownsville to anyone as a hometown, and since my dad has been mayor for the last few years, I know it is even better, and going places in the future!

And yet, it's not where you grow up that matters; rather it's how you are raised and with whom you grow up that makes the difference. You see, I had a very average start in life, maybe like many of you, but the important lesson is that where you are from—geographically or economically—does not limit your potential!

So, let me start at the beginning. I was born in San Antonio, Texas, and baptized as a member of St. Thomas More parish, the first child of loving parents with a mixed cultural heritage of American, Mexican, and German. Already, I was the standard "melting pot" product of immigrant families that form the backbone of America. Only sixteen months later, I got a little brother, Trey, and then later a sister, Melissa, and my youngest brother, Andy. Andy and I were the kids that grew up to look closest alike: great black hair, same handsome face, but he got the height I always wanted!

We didn't stay in San Antonio long before moving to Brownsville, where my dad set up his law firm. That's where I grew up, and that's where I call home.

I had a modest and "easy" life by most standards, but even so, it wasn't without some surprises, and the occasional stress. For example, when I was eleven years old, mom and dad got divorced, and with it came some confusion—awkwardness, sadness, and anger, mostly for Trey and me, as we were old enough to understand what was going on.

But then out of the suffering came some good, as we built special memories with each parent. "Mom time" was all about us four kids: she was tirelessly taking care of us so that we had a solid "comfort" foundation. Mom, especially, was a rock during tough times. "Dad time" was all about life lessons that have stayed with us since childhood. His focus was always us, even though he was, and still is, one of the busiest men I know, and we all loved the incredible "low budget" trips he would find for us. Then, there was a big awkward moment when, after a few years, our parents started dating other people. (As a young teenager, can you imagine your parents dating?!) But eventually, they both married some incredible people, and before long the tension and stress evaporated, and we reveled in the new people that had come into our lives.

Like I said, we are a very typical American family with many facets: white, Mexican, German, Polish, and we come complete with stepfathers, stepmothers, stepbrothers, and stepsisters. Growing up, we loved, laughed, and fought like any family would. And though divorce is not easy and certainly should be avoided, if possible, we also found some good in the situation—these great and wonderful people I now call my family. We are not a perfect family, of course; but happy and loving, yes. Nurturing all the children with good educational opportunities, and providing a firm foundation in the Church, absolutely! We were typical of many families in this complex, busy, and imperfect world; as I have come to call us, "the all-American family"—one I wouldn't trade for anything.

You can probably see from my background that your family, like mine, may not offer a straight or easy path to happiness. The same is true about the path to finding your passion and life's work. It may comfort you to know that my path was winding and rocky. So, don't get discouraged!

There is so much of my life that led me to a leadership role at Cristo Rey Jesuit, but I never would have guessed that was where the path would lead.

First, you may be surprised that I was the drum major of our school band; that's right, the person with the big stick that leads the marching band! Even at a young age, I enjoyed music. Mrs. Clare Hardee was my elementary school music teacher; she thought I could be a brilliant musician, and took me under her wing and began teaching me to play the piano. Music became a joyful and important part of my life, and looking back, I now see more clearly how it prepared me to lead in an engaging, even entertaining, way that I hope has inspired others, especially those associated with Cristo Rey Jesuit.

My parents encouraged this passion for music, and urged me to join the band in elementary school. I played the clarinet in the band, and a rather mean one too! My love for music carried into high school, where, of course, the sport that got all the attention was football—and I'm way, way too small to play—especially in Texas, where everything (and most certainly high school football) is done on a grand scale. But I had my eye on Leticia Hinojosa and her role leading the marching band. She was a graduating senior who commanded the utmost fear and respect from the band, and since she would be leaving, the spot was up for grabs. But I would only be a sophomore, so I thought I had little chance. I tried out anyway and gave it my best shot. And guess what! I became the next St. Joseph's Academy Fighting Bloodhound Drum Major!

The band wowed the crowd at football games; then we started wowing the crowds in local parades and even ended up on the front page of our local paper. I wasn't playing the clarinet anymore, but was sort of the director of the band while it was marching, and most certainly its biggest cheerleader. As I look back on that experience, I can see now that it is the very job that I have had these past few years at Cristo Rey Jesuit; as president, I was sort of the director (with a great deal of help), but the best part of my job has been as a huge cheerleader for each of you.

I still get a thrill out of being in the middle of the parade! I remember when First Lady Laura Bush came to our school in 2010 and gave a speech to five hundred students, teachers, administrators, and supporters, and said, "Cristo Rey Jesuit is now the sun that is rising over the southeast side of Houston....These students are learning values that will guide them in the years ahead—respect, perseverance, and integrity...most importantly, they are learning who they are and who they can be." I liked to summarize it simply as going "from the *barrio* to the boardroom." In doing so, you are shattering the perception, the false notion, that children growing up in poverty have neither the skill set nor ambition to work their way to success. I love being a cheerleader for the school and "drum majoring" that message to the rest of the city of Houston. And I still love being in the parade. Whenever I was tired and overwhelmed by the numbers, the finances, the spending, the fundraising, the strategic planning, I would put it all aside and walk out of my office door, and dive into the ocean of kids—the favorite part of my day!

Whether in high school as the band's drum major or at Cristo Rey Jesuit as president, I love to be right in the middle of everything, and I've often thought to myself, "I'm the luckiest Jesuit priest in the country."

After high school came Boston College and a degree in political science. Dad wanted each of us to "go east" for college to broaden our horizons, and we were fortunate to be able to afford to do it. But at Boston College, a seed was planted that would sprout much later. Being at a Jesuit college, I naturally received some history about various Catholic religious orders, including the Jesuit order with their focus on missionary work and education. The two mottos of Boston College—"Ever to Excel" and "Men and Women for Others"—impacted my subconscious as well, directing me toward what was to come.

One of my favorite teachers, Dr. Dorman Picklesmier, who taught speech class, invited me to be his teaching assistant. He thought the way I spoke should be taught to others. Wow! Can you imagine how good I felt—especially coming from Brownsville, Texas, with my Tex-Mex background. I was really inspired!

After graduating from college, I took a year-long volunteer job at an inner-city school in the Bronx, New York; this then allowed me to attend law school with my brother Trey, one of the most enjoyable educational interludes of my life—brothers rooming together and taking the same classes together. At that time, my initial plan was to become a lawyer and eventually work with my dad's firm in Brownsville. He had promised us jobs, provided our grades were good enough for him! But the seed planted in my mind at Boston College and nurtured during my volunteer work in New York City was beginning to grow.

Law school at the University of Texas was great. There were so many new things to learn quickly, not to mention a little "healthy competition" with my brother Trey, as a classmate and roommate. But suddenly, without much warning, a second plan emerged. One night, I woke up during my second year in law school at 2 a.m. and said, "I have to go to Mass." I went to the local Catholic Church to pray, and it felt amazing. The next day, I returned to the church with this *desperate* need to go to Mass. It stirred old thoughts from earlier in my life of joining the priesthood, that, unbeknownst to me, had been reignited at Boston College. So, I went on a retreat with the Oblates of Mary Immaculate, because I had grown up around members of the Oblate Order in South Texas. After the retreat, I was stunned to be told by the vocation director that I was not a "good fit" for the Oblates—but that I was meant to be a Jesuit! He was right, of course, and after completing law school, I joined the Society of Jesus.

The pathway to God, in my experience, has always been about following the crooked lines in the right way.

"Plan B" was now the path for me. The plan for my religious life was now in place!

Even my path along the religious life has not always been certain. More education is a big part of Jesuit formation, and I was blessed with some awesome teachers along the way. Father Paul Harman, SJ, was the director of the First Studies program at Loyola University, and became an incredible mentor and a good friend. He was instrumental in developing my leadership skills by "pushing" me into the role of student leader for all the Jesuit scholars. Little did I know at the time the importance of that experience for later at Cristo Rey Jesuit of Houston. Likewise, Father Dan Harrington, SJ, and Sister Meg Guider were two of my favorite professors in theology at Weston Seminary in Boston, where I took every one of their classes. They constantly encouraged me to continue theology studies, and even suggested that I take a doctorate and return to the seminary as a professor myself. I could really see that as a wonderful life: being a teacher.

Certainly, I was tempted with doctoral degree opportunities in both philosophy *and* theology before being sent by my Jesuit superiors to Harvard to study education. Going to Harvard was awesome. I was amazed as I perused the professors and course offerings, knowing that I would be taught by the leading researchers and practitioners in the field. It felt like being a kid in a candy store, with the most painful part of choosing not being able to choose *everything*. But there were only so many hours in the day, and alas, I was unable to alter the time!

At Harvard's educational leadership program, I got courses and skills that were directly relevant to leading Cristo Rey Jesuit, even though I didn't know that was where I was headed. The Harvard program introduced me to a new way of teaching and leading a school. With a mission statement in one hand and a business plan in the other, Harvard showed me how to be an engaging, fun-loving, strategic educator. Shared and distributed leadership—a major theme trumpeted by every professor at Harvard—both inspired me and gave me a new framework to understand and reenvision the very nature of how schools ought to operate. And just in time too, for just twenty-four hours after I graduated, I was on the airplane for Houston and my new life at Cristo Rey Jesuit.

Many of you already know the rest of the story. The last six years, when you all entered my life—the next "all-American" generation—allowed me to participate in what my Boston College professors always told me was the whole point of education: "to give back, to leave the world better than you found it, to help those who cannot help themselves."

It has been a great journey!

10
FINDING
ACCEPTANCE

Just so you know, I'm not perfect! And sometimes those closest to you are the best ones to remind us of our shortcomings.

You never see yourself precisely as others see you, and that is especially true of what I call a "brother's perspective"—the view of a brother, sister, or a particularly close friend. I am blessed to have two brothers and a sister—Trey, Andy, and Melissa—and they claim their insights about me are more accurate than my own memory, and, I might add, a bit less forgiving! They are undoubtedly right.

One of the joys of the last few months has been the company of my family as I have tried to cope with cancer. They have all been wonderful, attentive, and caring, each disrupting their own busy life to be with me when they can.

But there is a special bond with siblings—brothers and sisters—that conjures up a unique mixture of love and honesty you might not find with the rest of the family or friends. Both Trey and Andy have put their lives on hold for me, and essentially moved to Houston to care for me daily. And they have done more. On our daily walks, they have begun to tell me what life was like growing up with me! And when Melissa's medical practice in San Antonio allowed her to come to town, she did the same. This is a perspective I had never heard before. Being the eldest child, I had assumed I was almost perfect; but they tell a slightly different story!

Sometimes, these conversations during our walks even got into edgy ground, but ultimately, they reveal how much they admire and love me as a brother, despite my many faults and shortcomings. Through this activity, our relationship has grown closer at an important time in my life, for which I am eternally grateful. It has also made me a little humbler—and that's not a bad thing!

First, there's a humorous story about something that happened when I was a little kid, maybe nine years old. It is possible that I would have told you this story later in our lives, but maybe not; so, thank Trey for jogging my memory. The bottom line of the story is that I first conducted Mass when I was a kid in my bedroom—unofficially of course—and maybe this formed the origin of my enjoyment of saying Mass in people's homes, as was often done throughout Catholic history. This event occurred a year or so after receiving my first communion. Thus, I had in my possession my first holy communion book, with all the words of the Mass, including those said by the priest. Trey and I shared a room, and one Sunday morning we arranged our twin beds and two dresser drawers to form a U-shaped sanctuary, with a small kids' table in the far end as an altar, and the dresser drawers to be used as a tabernacle to hold the Eucharist. We smashed some ButterKrust bread into hosts, filled a glass with grape juice, and were ready to go. After pulling in some dining room chairs, Trey, my first altar boy, dutifully invited mom and dad to attend. When all were present, I opened the book and began right where I do today as a fully ordained priest: "In the name of the

Father, and of the Son, and of the Holy Spirit." Maybe God had started me on my journey already!

Another story dates from law school, and while my brothers found this terribly funny, in my defense let me say it happened at a very transitional time of my life when I had finally decided I would go into the priesthood after graduating. Anyway, that's my excuse! One evening at a dinner with Andy and Trey and some friends here in Houston, someone asked my brothers, "Tell us a story about Father T.J. that only you would know as his brother." "Yikes," I thought, "where was this going to lead?" They proceeded to tell a story to demonstrate a slight fault of mine: that I am perhaps a bit naïve. I have always described it as unabashed optimism, but they may have a point!

One cold, rainy day in Austin, there was a knock on our apartment door—the place that Trey and I shared during law school. Austin had its share of panhandlers and homeless that you would encounter, and we often just gave them money to let them be on their way. But on this day, I answered the door to this older gentleman, who stood there with what seemed to be panic in his eyes as he explained, "Please sir, I don't mean to bother you, but my daughter is sick and I am trying to get her to the doctor, and I have run out of gas. Could I borrow some money?" I immediately jumped into action, told him to wait a second, and got my jacket, ready to drive him and his daughter to the doctor. But he put his hands up to stop me, saying, "But I only need some money, and then I can get some gas." But I was already on a mission, and rushed past him telling him to hurry up so we could fetch his daughter. And then something amazing happened. He quickly ran away! I was astonished and couldn't believe what had just happened and returned to our apartment and told Trey, "I guess he didn't believe I had a car." Trey broke out laughing at me! Then I got it! There was no daughter, and there was no doctor to go to; he was just scamming for some money. Naïve? Yes, a little! But I am sure we would have given him some money anyway had he stayed around.

Of course, there are some "bad boy" stories, and my brothers have been relentless in reminding me of some of these on our walks. "Bandera shots" is one of them. There's not all that much to *do* in Brownsville, Texas, so as teenagers we would sometimes get creative, or maybe a bit too adventurous, and sneak over the border with some of our high school friends for some drinks—the alcoholic kind! One of them was the Bandera shot, and it's not a drink for the weak. It's a triple-layered drink that goes from a lime tasting, margarita-mix-like shot to the potent silver tequila shot to the bright red, spicy, and thick tomato juice shot. Altogether, it's a huge drink to take, uniquely Mexican— same colors as the flag—and you down it in one shot! Certainly, it was wrong, and I don't recommend it, of course! We were lucky to survive.

Even though my sister Melissa is the serious one among us, she has not left me unscathed! She reminded me recently that I could have—just maybe—a little streak of vanity. Mel, as we call her, is a world-class doctor, a psychiatrist. Really, nothing much gets past her. As her brothers, we always thought she was the smartest of the bunch. The vanity, she says, shows up in my hair care, and my muscles—I always liked to work out. But I have explanations! I like to dress properly for any occasion, and hair care is just a part of this desire. Wearing my hair a little longer than some may think appropriate, or spiking it up with gel, just made me feel more like you guys. Besides, I sense you liked it, at least judging by the number of guys that came by my office to borrow my hair gel! And, I might add, it's not just me that perpetuates this myth of my "iconic hair." Early in my chemotherapy treatment, a very dear friend sent me an e-mail to cheer me up: "Be strong and keep your hair flowing!" It made me smile.

As for the obsessive focus on working out, it's true! I started jogging in high school for exercise and continued this through law school and into my Jesuit training. At Dallas Jesuit, I coached the cross-country team and even ran along with the boys, worked in a few marathons, and began to supplement that with a weight lifting routine, sometimes consuming up to three hours with exercise. But I have a good excuse: I owe it all to my junior high school teacher Maureen Casteine, who told me on great authority that when you go to heaven, you go in your best human form. So, you see, plenty of exercise and hair gel—it only makes sense!

But that's enough of the funny stories! Here's a more serious one raised by my brothers on one of our walks, at a time when "serious" was the mood of the day. I was coping with chemotherapy and deciding how much longer to keep up a treatment that wasn't working, and worse, was destroying the life I had remaining. They told me, lovingly, that I was perhaps a bit too stoic and stubborn, and closed off emotionally. Of course, everyone was trying to help me figure out how to "beat this cancer," and I loved the help and suggestions, but, to a certain extent, it was something I needed to figure out on my own. I wanted answers, too, but primarily, it was to discern God's will for me in this situation. Certainly, part of that process was listening to my brothers, as God worked through them, but a part of the process also involved what we call in our Jesuit training an "attitude of indifference" to the options before me, and to try as best as possible to listen objectively to the clues. To achieve this, I needed, at times, to widen the emotional gap between us to "shield" myself to get through what was to come.

Stubborn, stoic, unemotional! How wonderful it is to have people in your life who can speak directly to your face, and then lovingly *accept* you!

Understanding who you are—who you *really* are—sometimes takes more than mere self-evaluation; it might take some listening to others as well. Family and good friends can be honest and direct; but in the process, they can help keep you humble, with a perspective of yourself that you might otherwise not see. It's worth checking out!

PART V

THE
SPIRITUAL SIDE

Antonio Martinez Jr., SJ

Ordained a Priest

June 9, 2007

For you, in fact, I am a bishop, with you I am a Christian.

—St. Augustine of Hippo, *Serm.* 340, 1;
PL 38, 1483

11
THE THREE ABSOLUTES

I am not an "accidental priest." My spiritual life as a Christian and as a priest is what defines me. It is the life I chose. It is my calling. For me, it is God's will.

Yet, my spiritual life is a constant struggle to navigate between the human experiences where you and I meet to accomplish some worldly task and the spiritual enterprise of discerning and doing God's will. Pierre Teilhard de Chardin, a famous twentieth-century French philosopher and Jesuit priest, put it this way: "We are not human beings having a spiritual experience. We are spiritual beings having a human experience." I love this quote because it captures the essence of the struggle we endure in trying to be a true companion of Jesus, and to integrate his mission into our daily lives—lives that we so easily and quickly clutter with the minutiae of our worldly human enterprise.

For many of you, my Roman Catholic faith may not be of interest. We never made religion a prerequisite for attending Cristo Rey Jesuit; and indeed, we welcome and respect *all* points of view. That is the Jesuit tradition. But to truly *know* me—as you would have in a longer life together—you would have caught a glimpse of my spirituality. Maybe that experience would illuminate your own spiritual existence, and give greater purpose to your human endeavors, as it surely has for me.

So, let's walk together for a moment as spiritual beings sharing a human experience, and I'll show you what I mean by tapping into your spiritual side. It's a story of the strength of faith available to each of you, if you want it; a story of understanding the gift of life, including the suffering and death that are part of our human existence.

My Jesuit brothers are an important part of my spiritual life and are my spiritual family. Just when I think I know it all, I am often challenged by one of them to think more deeply, or to pray with more insight to discern God's will, or encouraged to search harder to find God in all things.

Father Brian Reedy is one such brother. He has been our chaplain at Cristo Rey Jesuit, and was recently ordered to Rome for further studies. He has developed a unique insight into our spiritual lives that I find refreshing. He calls it the "Three Absolutes."

I can hear him speaking now, as he often did while relaxing outside after dinner, confidently distilling our broad mission as Jesuits into convenient categories and methodologies by which we might better discern God's will. Father Reedy and I often disagreed and had many spirited discussions. He's a scientist and finds comfort in "rules and regulations"—a human-created, natural order. But here, I think he's got it just right. He states,

> The three absolutes that all Jesuits hold true are: First, we are called to grow in faith, hope, and love. Second, we are called to participate in God's work of redemption—and for Jesuits that includes the various vows we take. And third, we are to share the good news of the Gospel, understanding and

letting others know that there is no reason to fear anything, not even death.

That's powerful stuff! This simple way of stating our Jesuit mission became a part of my thinking as I faced a troubling decision: whether to stop the aggressive chemotherapy that was making me so sick that life didn't feel like living or to continue treatments, and maybe—only maybe— add a little time to my existence. I wanted to be as sure as possible that my decision to stop the treatments, that clearly were not working anyway, was indeed God's will for me—and not just "T.J.'s will."

Thinking about these "Three Absolutes" has awakened my spiritual existence, and that, in turn, has allowed me to guide my human endeavors in a better way, a way that I believe conforms to God's will for me. Maybe it will help you too!

Believe me, I sometimes have trouble keeping my worldly activities on the right track. I can be impatient, stubborn, and sometimes have serious doubts. In short, I can be very human, with all the faults that come with that existence. But my spiritual side can come to the rescue, if I let it. And if I do, if I encourage that spiritual perspective in my life, I find purpose; I find redemption from my worldly errors, and I find peace.

For example, take the powerful admonition of Father Reedy's third absolute: "Understanding and letting others know there is no reason to fear anything, not even death." Wow! Conquering fear, conquering even the fear of death. It has worked for me, and perhaps the best way to explain how it has helped me is by focusing on a topic that I have learned a great deal about in the last year, and that is *suffering*. Suffering is part of the human condition, even though we quite naturally don't like it in any form.

Take, for instance, the natural suffering that comes with life. De Chardin, our Jesuit philosopher, has a wonderful way of capturing the essence of the gradual onset of suffering endured from the maladies of age as we grow old: "Growing old is like being increasingly penalized for a crime you haven't committed." I don't expect you as young people to really feel it; even at age forty-four, I didn't. But if you look carefully, you can see the frustration in older people as they have to accept the gradual degradation of their human body: you can't run as fast, there are more health issues, and maybe your memory gets a little faulty. This is suffering, but it is a natural part of life that we learn to live with and accept. I'm even told by many older people—because I never considered myself in that category—that the added wisdom that comes with age is worth the physical decline.

But what about suffering on a much larger scale: hunger, poverty, violence, injury, injustice, and sickness? What about suffering visited on innocent children? When we witness it, we feel sorry for the afflicted, and sometimes even try to help. But these too, unfortunately, seem to be common parts of life, though much harder to accept: the consequences are harsh, even life-threatening, the pain is too real to ignore, the hurt too deep to accept without question. And it's not just when these things happen to you. You suffer too when these things happen to your loved ones—maybe even more than they—or when they happen to the innocent and defenseless of the world.

So, *why does God let that happen?* What possible good can come from all this suffering? These are fair questions. Given my diagnosis of incurable cancer a few months ago, it is a timely topic for me, but it's also a very timeless topic.

Underlying my examination of the purpose and meaning of my own suffering is my belief in who we are as individuals—who we are as human beings. The truth is that our lives are not our own. We are gifts; my own life is a gift. I don't own it, I didn't create it, and I certainly don't have the control that I sometimes think I have over it, or, for that matter, that others think I have over it. *We belong to God*. We fall in line with God, as St. Ignatius constantly said about his Jesuits and those who are taught by Jesuits. We fall in line with God so that we can follow his will for our life. And ultimately, we give ourselves as gifts to God.

But suffering feels like a different thing. It doesn't *seem* like a gift, either to yourself or to those who love you and have to watch your suffering.

You might believe, as many do, that the gift of life is just the happy moments, the joyful moments, and that there is no gift in terms of pain and suffering. This is wrong—not just because I am Catholic, but because it is a comment on our human existence. God does not cause suffering, but I do believe that suffering is part of who we are.

The book *When Bad Things Happen to Good People* was written by a Jewish rabbi, Harold S. Kushner, and is incredibly thought-provoking. Rabbi Kushner tried to answer for himself the very personal question about what is the purpose of suffering in the context of his own daughter's incurable disease, and of course, while also trying to reconcile the incredible suffering of over six million Jews and others in the Shoah. In the final analysis, he poses the issue of finding purpose in suffering by looking to the future, and I think that works.

For me, the Jewish question, which is also the Catholic question, and which I think is the right question, is not "Why do we suffer?" It is "Where is God in this suffering?" That is the right question to ask. In asking that question, suffering becomes a statement of meaning, a statement of worth, a statement of gift.

What I am doing, here, is redefining the concept of *gift* to include suffering. It is part of the gift of life that I see reflected in the life of Christ, who is the *model*—not just for Catholics, but for *all* human beings—the model of redeemed suffering.

When I reflect on my own suffering and the suffering of the world—and again, not that God *causes* it, and not that any of us *wants* it—I see it as part of our life. I believe that there is something *redemptive* about suffering—what I and other people are going through—and that the suffering somehow allows us to share in the suffering of Christ. And because we share in the suffering of Christ, there is something salvific happening in this suffering, something mystically redemptive, as St. John Paul II wrote in his apostolic letter, *Salvifici Doloris*.

Our culture has separated suffering and salvation to such an extent that people no longer see it as worthy, or redemptive, or as a necessary part of being human. Maybe I want to connect these two again. Not only because I *believe* it, but also because my faith informs it and because it is *real*.

But I'm a Christian. What about those people who don't believe in Christ as Savior? Maybe they see him as just a great guy or a great moral teacher and don't feel like they *need* to be saved.

Even then, the facts of human existence point to a natural good that can come from suffering, if we look for it. Immediately after an age of suffering follows an age of *reverence*. For example, following the horrific event of 9/11, there was an age of reverence. Because of 9/11, we revered each other a little more, the country became more united, and we revered our rights and responsibilities more, and our children. There was an outpouring of love that wasn't there before, a sense of honor and respect that had been dormant was openly expressed, and praise more often took the place of criticism.

I also saw this in a very small way when I got to Houston to start Cristo Rey Jesuit. Within two weeks of buying a property to start the school, we were hit by Hurricane Ike, and for the next two weeks, we were out of power. This was minor suffering compared to 9/11, but what was fascinating was that, in this minor event of suffering, people started to pay more attention—just a little bit more—to their neighbor. People started talking to each other, people invited other people to see each other, people shared their food with each other, people treated each other as *people*—beings with the dignity that God instilled in us from the beginning.

Suffering is ultimately transformed into reverence: an ability to love one another more and an ability to love God because of the suffering. I certainly see it in my own situation: thousands of people have sent letters and e-mails to pray for my health. The community at Cristo Rey Jesuit has never been tighter, and the supporters of Cristo Rey Jesuit have never been more generous. There is something happening, because of what I am going through, that the kids at Cristo Rey Jesuit will benefit from. So, yes, through the suffering and pain, you find reverence and community building. You find bonding and faith escalating moments happening. And that only happens in our most difficult times.

You might ask, Has my own experience in suffering changed the way I see God, and has it caused any difficult moments in my own journey of faith? Of course, but I also see certain things more clearly.

First, it has made me more sensitive to other people who are suffering, and to acknowledging the "unfairness" in my situation. But that unfairness does not necessarily challenge my faith and love for God, because things can be unfair while I'm still in love with God.

Again, I don't believe that God is the *cause* of suffering, but I do believe that suffering has meaning. There is a larger picture than what we can see, and my faith tells me that God will take my suffering, and the suffering of the whole world, and somehow use it in a way that becomes a saving moment—not just for humanity, but for us as individuals as well. Therefore, given this, my love for God has *not* changed.

But there are more questions that arise in my own mind. Some days are harder; others are easier. It is very difficult to watch my ability to eat diminish to almost nothing because of the cancer ravaging throughout my body. However, at the same time, as I am praying, doing my Examination of Conscience, celebrating Mass, each of these amazing moments becomes more pregnant and poignant than ever before.

Rather than the now irrelevant five-year strategic plan, life is now minute-to-minute. And therefore, God is more readily available and much more present to me, because I am much more present to him. That reverencing part is far clearer. I am more attentive to the God of the here and now, and that becomes a powerful moment in prayer, and certainly deepens my relationship with Christ.

There is a larger picture that none of us has a right to see or even to understand. My suffering is *not* just tough on me; it's tougher on other people. Watching someone you love suffer is harder than suffering. But what I always tell them—those who suffer because of my suffering—is that the story is going to end well. Just look at what we accomplished at Cristo Rey Jesuit together! My story is part of a larger story, and *it will end well*. God has the bigger picture,

God has the grander story, and I love God enough to know that picture will win in the end.

As human beings, we don't necessarily understand "God's calculus," but by *accepting* our spiritual existence we can glimpse the possibility of a bigger picture. Our Jesuit documents tell us, "From the beginning of our formation and throughout our lives, we must be and remain familiar with the things of God. Our desire to grow now and in the future in the 'interior' knowledge of Our Lord, who became human for me, that I may love him more intensely and follow him more closely." Thus, as a spiritual being, I trust the power of the risen Christ—I fear nothing now, not even death.

Therefore, the "Three Absolutes" can help illuminate your spiritual existence: grow in faith, hope, and love; participate in God's work of redemption; share the good news of the gospel; and learn to fear nothing, not even death. Awakening your spiritual side will make your life at least *twice* as good!

Of course, what *you* believe must be *your* choice. Just know that I will be with you regardless of your personal decision. At my ordination as a priest, I embraced the admonition of St. Augustine, and I promise to follow it for each of you: so, if I walk with you only in our human experience, know that I join you as a Christian; but if you join me in a spiritual life, know that I am here for you as a priest.

12
TAKE, LORD, AND RECEIVE

In the name of the Father, and of the Son, and of the Holy Spirit, Amen!

I am nearing the end of my journey with you, so it seems appropriate to discuss larger issues—matters that are more important in helping you live a full life, and demonstrate what I've said from the beginning: the story will end well for me. I invite you now to share in my faith that makes this so.

These are not the tips or life experiences that will help you get a better test grade or earn your college degree or get a good job. We have talked about those things already. The questions we will consider now often dwell in the shadows of your mind as you navigate through your busy world. You think about them sometimes and know they are there, but mostly they remain mute and hidden from daily scrutiny.

But these "larger issues" are the ones that feed your soul: Do you really need to believe? Do you really need to pray? Do you really matter?

When you think about them, even in passing, they force you to confront what it means to be human; they expose our human limitations. My relationship with you began with "your education"—high school, college, career.

Beyond these worldly limitations, let's now discuss the bigger picture of what I believe is God's plan, in which we all play an important part.

These are truly amazing questions! But most of us don't give them much thought. We have more pressing worries: where to get our next meal, studying for an exam, building our foundations for a good career and a happy life. But, I wonder, are these truly enough? Does our soul need more?

Three years ago, I met a gentleman at a charity function. He seemed to be searching for and wanting something more. Over the next few months, we talked about these questions, sometimes over hamburgers at lunch. He soon decided to join the Church; in fact, he became my first convert to the faith. Such is the power of these issues I want to discuss with you now!

The essence of our discussion was the seemingly hopeless limitations of the educated human mind to comprehend the reason for human existence. But then we considered that rather than logic or scientific proof, why wouldn't it be just as reasonable to conclude that it is the "mystery of our faith" that provides the answers to these questions? After all, how much more interesting does this mystery make our universe: one we cannot comprehend with our limited capabilities; one governed by a calculus beyond our logic and reason, and totally beyond our imagination? Perhaps God's bigger picture can only be appreciated through the medium of faith.

This is *not* a vague notion of God as merely a gap-filler between what we know—information gathered as the fabric of our reality is slowly revealed through the eons of human education—and those yet unanswered questions. God is much more than that—too big for us to fully comprehend with our limited intellectual prowess.

The "mystery of faith" allows us to glimpse the unimaginable, even as we continue to probe the vastness of creation with our limited human intellectual capabilities. It allows us to find meaning and purpose in our lives, even as we come to understand our seemingly miniscule place in the fabric of the universe. It allows us to reconcile suffering, evil, and goodness in a complex world. In short, it allows us to find God in everything.

One of my Jesuit brothers, Father James Martin, tells a story that is worth repeating. In fact, many of his stories are worth repeating! But the story he tells that is important here is about the atheist caught in a flood who decides that the flood threatening his house is the chance to prove whether God exists. Essentially, he dares God to reveal himself and to save him:

> The atheist caught in the flood says to himself, "If there is a God, I will ask him for help, and he will save me." When he hears a warning on the radio, advising listeners to move to higher ground, he ignores it. "If there is a God, he will save me," he thinks. Next, a firefighter knocks on his door to warn him to evacuate. "If there is a God, he will save me," he says to the firefighter. When the floodwaters rise, the man climbs to the second floor. The Coast Guard boat motors by his window and offers him rescue. "If there is a God, he will save me," he says and refuses help from the Coast Guard.
>
> Finally, he ends up on the roof, with the waters rising around him. A police helicopter hovers over the house and drops a rope to climb. "If there is a God, he will save me!" he shouts over the roar of the helicopter's blades.

Suddenly, a giant wave sweeps over him, and the man drowns and finds himself in heaven. When God comes to welcome him, the atheist is at first surprised. And then, furious. "Why didn't you save me?" he asks.

"What do you mean?" says God. "I sent the firefighter, the Coast Guard, and the police officer, and you still wouldn't listen!"

Some people refuse to listen, unless God reveals himself on *our* terms! And even when he did, through Jesus Christ, many couldn't hear him. But through the act of prayer, you can learn to communicate with God in ways that defy the laws of nature, as we know them. Prayer is a conversation with God, and how you do it and where you do it is unique to you. But make no mistake, it isn't necessarily always easy and it requires commitment. And, as our atheist friend in Father Martin's story found out, you need to listen very carefully! We may even know the messenger, as he did, and because of our inherent human limitations, still miss the message.

So, if the reality of God is beyond our imagination, why can't it be beyond what we so glibly call the "laws of nature?" Why can't it be the mystery of our faith—a mystery we embrace with our limited human capabilities as firmly as the things we can see and touch? Indeed, a mystery we embrace with our heart and soul when we imagine the unimaginable—a Creator that cares about each of us as individuals, even as we know we are smaller than a grain of sand among the billions of stars and other worlds in this universe.

At every communion, I try to say your name as I offer you the body of Christ. I don't know all who come forward, and even when I recognize a face, sometimes I don't succeed in remembering your name, but God does! And the Lord said, "I have called you by name, you are mine" (Isa 43:1). In the vastness of the cosmos, God calls you by your name! It's not illogical; it's just unimaginable with our limited intellectual capabilities.

Recently, I began to feel the fatigue of cancer. So, I wrote to my first convert and said, "You'll *never* know how deeply grateful I am to you for your passion and expertise. As my one and only convert, you are and always will be super, super special!" It was the first time I had mentioned that he might be my only convert to the faith, and I know it made him uncomfortable; not because he knew I was dying—he knew that—but I think because he was nervous about being the only one. Way too much pressure! So, I won't be disappointed if others that I have been privileged to know in this life follow in his footsteps—he needs company!

Ultimately, it's *your* choice how you respond to the bigger issues. No, you don't need to *believe*; you don't need to *pray*, and you can conclude that, in the vastness of the universe, we don't *really* matter. But your life will be richer if you answer yes, in your own way, to each of these. If you do, I can promise that you will find purpose, peace, and a full life. This is the mystery of our faith!

As for me, I made my decision long ago, and I am filled with joy every day because of it. I know now that I will not have a long life, but trust me when I tell you it has been a full one. In fact, Father James Martin raised this issue with me last summer after I had received my diagnosis. He asked me whether I thought about death. What a question! And how thankful I am that he knew me well enough to ask.

I told him that I do think about it, especially at night when I am alone with my thoughts, but I don't *dwell* on it. I added, that it amazes me that I can even find God in this journey. In some ways, this was the perfect time for this to happen.

Remarkably, my incurable cancer diagnosis came just after completing tertianship, the last stage of Jesuit formation, on a six-month mission in East Africa. There, I had witnessed the confluence of suffering and joy in a way that I had not imagined possible. Then, in preparation for taking my final vows, I made the final prayer, the *Suscipe*, from the *Spiritual Exercises of St. Ignatius*, as an offering to God:

> *Take, Lord, and receive all my liberty,*
> *my memory, my understanding, and my entire will—*
> *all that I have and possess.*
> *You, Lord, have given all to me.*
> *To You, O Lord, I return it.*
> *All of it is yours.*
> *Dispose of it wholly according to your will.*
> *Give me Your love and Your grace,*
> *for that is enough for me.*

I am ready. I am a Jesuit priest and Jesuits are always given a mission. So, if my mission from Jesus right now is to be sick, then I accept it. And if my mission is to die, then I accept that mission too.

The last six years of my life at Cristo Rey Jesuit of Houston have been my best assignment ever, but the next one will be even better: my soul in heaven with eternal life, watching over each of you, and, yes, praying for each of you! *Gracias a la vida!*

The story does end well, as I told you it would. Wherever my story ends, it's part of God's bigger picture. Even the suffering we endure together—mine and yours—finds purpose in bringing us closer. My story, your story, our story…is going to end well!

Praise be Jesus Christ, forever. Amen!

Appendix I

The Funeral Mass Homily

*The Most Reverend Joseph A. Fiorenza, Archbishop
Emeritus of the Archdiocese of Galveston-Houston
—Funeral Mass for Father T.J. Martinez, SJ, on
December 2, 2014.*

Six years ago, a young priest arrived here with the daunting
task of providing the poorest children of the city with a
renowned Jesuit education that would prepare them for
attending college. It was a huge challenge and he began from
ground zero. A work-study program for the children of the
poorest families existed in several cities, but it would begin
in Houston with a thirty-eight-year-old Jesuit, gifted with
enormous energy, a passion, and creative talents motivated
by a heartfelt love for the poor. But in no other city would
these special schools be so quickly and effectively successful
as Cristo Rey Jesuit of Houston.

Small in stature, Father Antonio Martinez, known as
Father T.J., was a giant of a man as he crisscrossed this
city seeking support for a new type of college preparatory school. With a contagious enthusiasm and a spellbind-
ing appeal for this new approach in education, he would

speak to anyone and before any group about preparing the poor for a college education. He spoke before the Greater Houston Partnership, the boards of financial and industrial corporations, law firms, parish groups, editorial boards, television stations, civic groups, women's clubs, anywhere he was invited. Houston embraced not only the work-study program of education for college, but the city embraced this young Jesuit with an infectious laugh, a booming voice, and the unique talent of making everyone he met feel like his special friend. In the few short years, he was like a brilliant comet streaking across Houston, giving light and life to all who came near his orbit, but exhausted with cancer, his earthly mission completed, like a comet he faded away.

T.J. was on a mission. The key to understanding him, or to use the scriptural term, the *hermeneutic* that unlocks the mystery of this man of unusual energy and perpetual enthusiasm, with a passionate desire to educate the students of Cristo Rey and his unrelenting promotion of the school, is found in his belief that he was sent to Houston for the same reason that his Jesuit founder, Ignatius Loyola, sent Francis Xavier five hundred years ago to India and the Far East: to bring the gospel message of salvation in Christ. T.J. understood that his assignment by his superior was the will of God, as in the gospel we just heard: Jesus came to do the will of the Father, and promised eternal life to those who believed in him as sent by the Father. Father T.J. deeply believed that he was sent to Houston to establish a special school, but basically, he came here to bring the teachings of Jesus to the poor and nonpoor alike. Without understanding this, T.J. is just another mystifying human phenomenon, but by understanding his mission in the proper context, we can see his mission here as a mystery in God's plan for him and for us.

His mission succeeded beyond what he even imagined.

This coming May, the third senior class will graduate. Like the previous two graduating classes, they will begin college with a Jesuit education. Without Cristo Rey Jesuit, it is doubtful if any of these graduates would have been able to attend college. Under Father T.J.'s influence, Cristo Rey not only prepares students for college but gives them confidence in themselves as capable of pursuing a college education, the confidence to become successful in whatever profession or vocation they choose.

A little more than two weeks ago, I visited T.J. His body was ravaged with cancer, but his mind was sharp and clear as a bell. We recalled special times we had enjoyed together. I thanked him for the gift he has been to the school, to the archdiocese, to Houston, and to his legion of friends. Then he said it all has been a great joy for him. These last six years, he said, have been good, the best for him. Then, with a smile, he said—as only someone who is at peace and near death can say—"My next assignment will really be good." He knew that after death there is a new and resurrected life in Christ, and that assignment would give him perfect joy and peace. In the midst of his horrific suffering, he had confidence that being united with Christ in his passion and death, he would be one with him in his resurrection.

Father T.J. was a good priest, a Jesuit disciple of Christ. He placed his great intelligence, his amazing and innovative mind, his gospel zeal and love for the poor, his wonderful sense of humor and special kindness and tenderness toward all as gifts in service to the Church he loved.

Shortly after receiving the brutal truth of cancer at an advanced stage, he wrote in a note to me with his amazing analytical, managerial mind, "I'm ready for plan B, whatever God wills that to be, even if it is going through the 'third week,' which is the passion and death of Christ, because I know the story will end well."

Only one who has lived life, with all its joys and sorrows, can surrender to God with the confidence that all will end well. Certainly, all ends well whenever we live and die believing in Jesus. T.J.'s life ended embracing the cross of Christ. On Thanksgiving evening, I visited him for the last time. He was in a coma, I thought. After praying the prayers for the dying for him with his mother and father, I blessed him with my cross and touched his forehead with it. Then I, rather instinctively, touched his lips with the cross and he puckered up his lips and kissed his crucified Christ. He knew what was happening. In dying, all was well.

The illness of Father T.J and his dying process was a graced moment not only for him but for all of us who witnessed his profoundly moving and beautiful acceptance of God's will. Thousands in Houston joined the Cristo Rey community in praying for a miraculous cure. We prayed to God that this charismatic and zealous priest who accomplished so much good for young people in a short span of time would be able to continue his mission for many years to come.

We know that God listens to our prayers, and he answers them in ways, even miraculous ways, which we do not envision. Both in life and in dying, Father T.J. was a grace for us. He was a teacher to the end, giving us the witness of how we are to embrace God's will and surrender our lives to his loving and providential care.

He died a young man and certainly he wanted to live much longer, to be able to continue helping children of low-income families prepare for college, to serve his Church in every way his superior decided. Once I heard him say that if he had his choice, he would like to be an epistemological theologian. I am sure he would have been a great one in the Jesuit tradition. But he lovingly accepted the obedience to start a special school in Houston for disadvantaged children.

His faith-filled dying reflected a strong belief in the resurrection promised to those who live a life for God and of loving service for all God's people. With the same spirit of religious obedience, he accepted his illness and faced approaching death with his eyes wide open, and he did not blink. He witnessed to the end how we are to live for Christ and how to die in Christ. He has helped each one of us to live a better life for others, more aware and more sensitive to the needs of the disadvantaged and marginalized.

I have lived in Houston for sixty years. I have *never* known a priest who in such a few years accomplished so much for so many. His legacy will live on in the lives of all the graduates and future graduates of Cristo Rey Jesuit. Whatever they may do as good and productive citizens can be traced back to a young Jesuit with enormous love and zeal who gave them the priceless gift of a college education. The solid foundation on which T.J. established Cristo Rey Jesuit assures that it will continue to be an outstanding educational institution for its students. In a short time, he imbued such a strong, deep love and spirit for this special school into the board of trustees, the administration and members of the faculty, and the many wonderful and generous supporters that Cristo Rey Jesuit will not just endure but will continue as an excellent college preparatory school. When challenges arise, as they will, recall the constant mantra of Father T.J.: *Let's do the difficult things first and the impossible soon after.*

I have not known of *anyone* who has had such a huge influence on Houston in just a few years. He not only quickly won the admiration of people from every section of this great city, but he left a vision of a city that values the education of all students, but especially of students from its poorest areas. He had the vision of these students becoming physicians, nurses, attorneys, research scientists, engineers, leaders of business and industries, teachers and college professors, members of Congress and economists. He gave us a transformative vision of a city that reflects the kingdom of God in which each person is respected, loved, and valued as a brother or sister. In six years, his vision has helped make Houston a better city for all its people. We should always be grateful to God for the unusual gift Father T.J. has been to Houston and to Cristo Rey Jesuit.

I offer my prayers and deep condolences to each member of the Martinez family, to his Jesuit brothers, to his coworkers at Cristo Rey Jesuit, to the students who were the love of his life, and to all his many, many friends in Houston and around the world.

Viva Cristo Rey!

APPENDIX II

Eulogies

EULOGY OF TREY, MELISSA, AND ANDY MARTINEZ

Our brother was dangerously unselfish. His life serves as a template for how we want to live—with an attitude of gratitude, praying for indifference to our selfish desires and dreams, and being open to God's will.

Time does not heal all wounds, but through suffering and pain we can find meaning. The sharp, stabbing pain and heaviness in our hearts have yielded to a dull ache that waxes and wanes depending on the circumstances. There was the unspoken, irrational hope that his death was not real. As we sort through our thoughts and emotions, searching for understanding and meaning, there is hope that we can transform our suffering into something positive and useful.

Time has also given us the opportunity to realize and appreciate what it took to launch and build a Cristo Rey school. We appreciate those who dedicated time, money, or both to support the vision.

We thank Paul Posoli, who took over as president of Cristo Rey after our brother was diagnosed with cancer. He exceeded T.J.'s expectations and solidified the direction of Cristo Rey for years to come. He is a living example of "Men and Women for Others." We also thank the City of Houston. Not only did you embrace and support our brother, you took him in as one of your own. The Martinez family is forever grateful.

To the past, present, and future graduating classes of Cristo Rey Houston, T.J. saw himself in each of you. We grew up in Brownsville, the poorest city in the nation, with parents that worked hard to provide their children with everything necessary to succeed—the opportunity to dream big!

Having T.J. as an older brother was a gift for which we thank God every day. While we miss his bright smile and boundless energy, we are grateful to have shared our lives with him. He approached every adventure with enthusiasm—even death, the greatest one of all.

EULOGY OF REVEREND TOM GREENE, SJ

I am Father Tom Greene, and I have the privilege of saying a few words on behalf of the Society of Jesus about my good friend, T.J. Martinez. Our friendship began in the novitiate, we were ordained together, and I was able to journey with him the past month until he died.

T.J. was an outstanding Jesuit, but he came to us as an outstanding person and for that we have to thank his wonderful family. Thank you!

This week's first reading of the Advent season reminded us that God is the potter and we are the clay. Well, God shapes us through the lives of others and we know T.J. was largely shaped by God's grace working through so many of the people here tonight. And so, the Society of Jesus is also deeply grateful to you. Thank you!

At last night's beautiful wake and rosary, there was a prayer card put together by Cristo Rey, which used the quote, "Go and Set the World on Fire," a quote that was used by St. Ignatius as he closed his letters. I chuckle when I see that quote because if you were to go to the Jesuit curia—headquarters—in Rome, you would find just inside the main entrance a statue of St. Ignatius with this inscription. And, whether through the oddities of the Italian fire code or someone's sense of humor, you would find tucked behind the statue a fire extinguisher! Well perhaps that is an apt image for our world. Our dreams can often be extinguished by other people or by our own doubts and fears. No doubt T.J. had them. But God's work cannot be extinguished, and T.J. was a five-alarm blaze that could not be put out. No criticism or cynicism or self-doubt could extinguish his dream of bringing Catholic education to South East Houston.

I took great pride in watching all that he accomplished over the years. Much has been made of T.J.'s ministry in Houston and all that he accomplished. I want to double down on that praise, I want to affirm it, I want to shout it from the rooftops. The media attention has focused on him as a man of action, and rightfully so. His legacy for the world is his active ministry of Cristo Rey. But, the accolades and recognition focus on his exterior life, his action, the external aspects of his life.

However, to be honest with you, that is not his greatest achievement for us as Jesuits. The Society of Jesus will remember him for something much more important, much more significant that won't receive a lot of media coverage—we will remember him for his interior life and for becoming a man of the *Spiritual Exercises*. Our Jesuit documents state that "from the beginning of our formation and throughout our lives, we must be and remain familiar with the things of God. Our desire is to grow now and in the future in the 'interior knowledge of Our Lord, who became human for me, that I may love him more intensely and follow him more closely.'"

The litmus test for this deepened relationship with the Lord is the *Suscipe*. The final prayer of the *Spiritual Exercises of St. Ignatius*. It is the prayer of ultimate and complete trust in God:

> *Take, Lord, and receive all my liberty,*
> *my memory, my understanding, and my entire will—*
> *all that I have and possess.*
> *You, Lord, have given all to me.*
> *To You, O Lord, I return it.*
> *All of it is yours.*
> *Dispose of it wholly according to your will.*
> *Give me Your love and Your grace,*
> *for that is enough for me.*

It's a beautiful prayer; until you truly begin to lose all that you have and possess, when you lose your health, limb by limb, when cancer invades your body...then it's hard to say that only God's love and grace are enough. But T.J. was able to say that prayer with conviction. He prayed it as fervently when healthy as he did near death. He prayed it as authentically when he was running six miles a day and when he could walk only six steps. He was peaceful and convinced that his flight was arriving on time as scheduled. He trusted God.

T.J. came to know the power of the risen Christ in whom he could place his full trust. And so the Society of Jesus will remember T.J. much more as a man who accepted the call of Christ and trusted God's plan for his life. He inspires the Society of Jesus by showing us that even today, after more than 450 years, our Ignatian spirituality is still valid and that young men still desire to serve under the banner of the Cross and live out the *Suscipe*.

Perhaps this might serve as a legacy for you. As the years pass and you drive down Highway 45 or Mt. Carmel Drive, or see a picture of T.J., our hope is that you see Cristo Rey not so much as the accomplishment of a man, but rather of what is possible if you develop a deep and trusting relationship with our Lord. That is the Society of Jesus' prayer for you. May God bless us, may God grant you this prayer.

A Final Prayer

The "Prayer for Generosity" of St. Ignatius Loyola is my favorite prayer because it applies to all of us, not just Catholics, and it encompasses what it means to be a human being. It derives from the Greek word for emptiness—*kenosis*—which in theological and philosophical terms has come to mean the "self-emptying" of one's own will in order to become entirely receptive to playing a part in a divine plan. This prayer totally corresponds with my understanding of our human nature as "giving" of self, which ultimately leads to deep, deep happiness and peace, whether it be starting a school for underprivileged kids, working as a missionary in Africa, being a great parent for your kids, or whatever inspires one to "empty yourself" in the service of others. It's powerful, it was given to us by St. Ignatius, and as an added bonus, it's short!

So, I offer this as a prayer for my only nephew Jason and my only niece Alyssa, and for all my students, family, and friends to use, in your own way, as you chart your course in life. *Know that I will be with you!*

In the name of the Father, and of the Son, and of the Holy Spirit:

Dearest Lord,
Teach me to be generous,
Teach me to serve as you deserve,

Miracle in Motion

To give and not to count the cost,
To fight and not to heed the wounds,
To toil and not to seek for rest,
To labor and not to ask for reward,
Save that of knowing that I am doing thy will. Amen!

Viva Cristo Rey! Viva Cristo Rey Jesuit!

                            Antonio Martinez Jr., SJ
                            November 6, 2014

Praise for
Miracle in Motion

At Cristo Rey Schools, students learn respect, commitment, integrity, and the importance of knowing who you are, and who you can become. Father Martinez lived a life based on these values, and I am grateful that his book will teach students for generations to come.

—Mrs. Laura Bush, first lady of the
United States of America, 2001–2009

It was a joy to work with Father T.J. Martinez as he labored to establish Cristo Rey Jesuit College Preparatory in Houston. He was an intelligent and hard-working priest with a passion for serving the poor, always living the words of St. Ignatius of Loyola—namely, to be a man for others. In his illness, he embodied the Suscipe: "Everything is yours; do with it what you will. Give me only your love and your grace, that is enough for me."

—His Eminence Daniel DiNardo, cardinal,
archbishop of Galveston-Houston, president of the
United States Conference of Catholic Bishops

Father T.J. Martinez continues his legacy through the pages of this book. His wise words move us, once more, to contemplate, appreciate, and persevere through life's adversities and triumphs. He was a truly unique and charismatic leader who inspired others to be a real force for good in the world.

—Rich and Nancy Kinder (Kinder Foundation)

This fine, tender, and edifying book is like Cristo Rey Jesuit and T.J. Martinez's life: All point beyond themselves to the God who loves us without measure and without regret. This book is a lasting gift for us all.

—Father Gregory J. Boyle, SJ, best-selling author of *Tattoos on the Heart* and founder of Homeboy Industries

Father T.J. Martinez's book is a reminder to all of us that the "American dream" of professional happiness is attainable through hard work, perseverance, and following the path of the right role models—choosing the right hero. Father T.J. is certainly a hero of mine!

—César Millan, best-selling author of *Lessons from the Pack* and host of the TV show *Dog Nation*

T.J. lived the motto he so frequently quoted: "We do the difficult immediately and the impossible right after." His spunk and spirit led him to undertake the difficult and stare down the impossible without flinching. T.J. willed us his enthusiasm and commitment, and he will always be "our man in heaven!"

—Father John Foley, SJ, founder, chair emeritus and
chief mission officer of the Cristo Rey Network)

Who am I to question God's actions? But I do wish that He would have left Father T.J. on planet Earth a little longer. What a fabulous priest, teacher, and American. I am thankful that our paths crossed.

—George W. Strake, Jr., Houston businessman,
philanthropist, and former Texas secretary of state

Father T.J. Martinez's contagious enthusiasm and courageous commitment in launching the next generation of education reform rested on creating a groundbreaking educational market where no son or daughter of Houston is left behind. His irrepressible spirit of hope—living with an "attitude of gratitude"—permeates the pages of this book. Gracias a la vida!

—Sofia Adrogué, Houston lawyer, author, and cohost
and coproducer of the TV show *Latina Voices: Smart Talk*